IMPRESSIONIST
—DRAWINGS—

♦

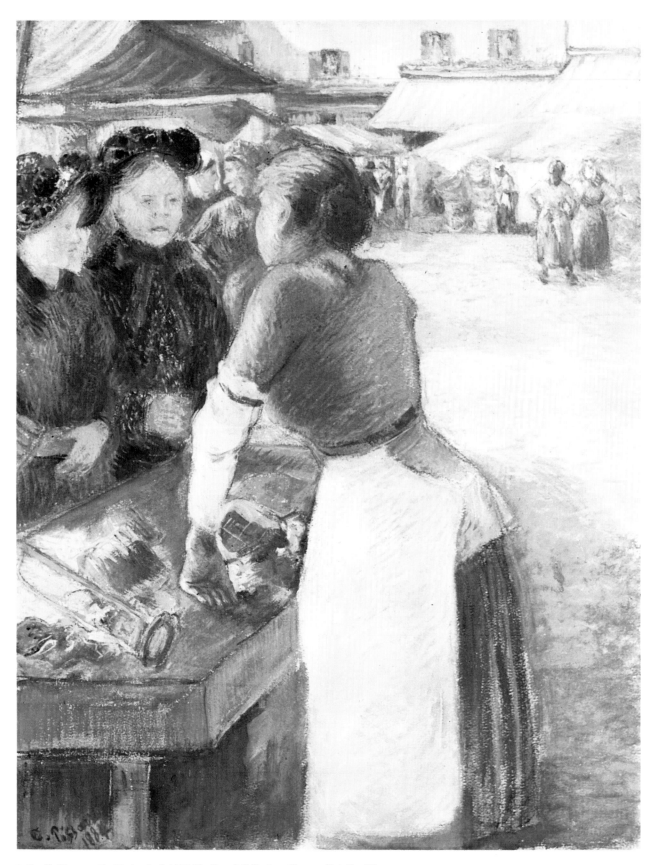

1 Camille Pissarro, *The Market Stall*. 1884. The Burrell Collection, Glasgow (Cat. No. 55).

IMPRESSIONIST
—DRAWINGS—

from British Public and Private Collections

◆

Christopher Lloyd
and
Richard Thomson

Phaidon Press and the Arts Council

an exhibition sponsored by

The Royal Bank
of Scotland plc

Ashmolean Museum, Oxford 11 March–20 April 1986
Manchester City Art Gallery 30 April–1 June 1986
The Burrell Collection, Glasgow 7 June–13 July 1986

Exhibition organized by Roger Malbert,
assisted by Lise Connellan

Phaidon Press Limited, Littlegate House,
St Ebbe's Street, Oxford OX1 1SQ

First published 1986
© The Arts Council of Great Britain 1986

British Library Cataloguing in Publication Data

 Lloyd, Christopher, 1945–
  Impressionist drawings : from British public and
  private collections.
  1. Drawing, French – Exhibitions
  2. Impressionism (Art) – France – Exhibitions
  I. Title II. Thomson, Richard
  741.944'074 NC246

  ISBN 0-7148-2418-6
  ISBN 0-7148-2419-4 Pbk

Printed in Great Britain by Balding + Mansell Limited

AUTHORS' ACKNOWLEDGEMENTS

We are indebted to a number of people for help and support
in the preparation of this exhibition. First and foremost, we
are extremely grateful to those museums and private
collectors who have agreed to lend drawings in their
possession. All those with whom we discussed the project
extended to us a warm welcome and with great tolerance, not
to say on occasions perhaps with quiet amusement, allowed
us to ferret through their collections.

 Jack Baer and Stefanie Maison gave invaluable advice and
assistance with the selection, thereby generously sharing
with us years of unrivalled experience in the field of
nineteenth-century French drawings. Special thanks are also
due to Antony Griffiths, John Rowlands, David Scrase and
Lady Stewart. Timothy Bathurst, Lilian Browse, William
Darby, Adrian Eeles and Thomas Gibson vigorously sup-
ported the idea of the exhibition and joined in the search for
drawings in private collections when our spirits flagged.
Others, such as Melanie Clore, Desmond Corcoran, David
Ellis-Jones, Frederick Mulder, Christian Neffe, Constance
Pemberton, Caroline Simon, Robert Stoppenbach, Michel
Strauss, William Weston and John Whately withstood
persistent questioning and several consultations with great
forbearance.

 Several scholars discussed individual drawings, or particular issues, with us during the course of our work on the
catalogue : Dr Keith Andrews, Frances Carey, Dr John House,
Professor Michael Kauffmann, Professor Theodore Reff,
Anne Thorold, Philip Vainker and Dr Jon Whiteley.

Christopher Lloyd
Richard Thomson

Contents

FOREWORD

Christopher Lloyd of the Ashmolean Museum and Richard Thomson of Manchester University proposed this exhibition of drawings by the Impressionists and other French artists of the last quarter of the nineteenth century. We are indebted to Mr Lloyd and Mr Thomson for the dedication with which they have made the selection and written the catalogue. The exhibition is drawn entirely from collections in this country and includes many drawings unknown to the public. We are most grateful to the lenders, whose generosity has made the exhibition possible.

Joanna Drew
Director of Art

LIST OF LENDERS

(references are to Catalogue numbers)

Bristol, City of Bristol Museum & Art Gallery	25, 70
Cambridge, the Syndics of the Fitzwilliam Museum	2, 5, 10, 16, 72
Cardiff, National Museum of Wales	8, 60
Dundee Art Galleries and Museums	17
Thomas Gibson Fine Art	12
Glasgow, The Burrell Collection	20, 21, 28, 35, 37, 39, 41, 55, 65, 80
Lord Goodman	27
London, the Trustees of the British Museum	6, 31, 32, 68, 74, 75, 76
London, Courtauld Institute Galleries	9, 34, 73
London, Victoria and Albert Museum	11, 33
Manchester, Whitworth Art Gallery, University of Manchester	22, 30, 57, 62
Oxford, the Visitors of The Ashmolean Museum	13, 14, 15, 19, 36, 38, 42, 43, 46, 47, 48, 50, 52, 53, 58, 59, 61a–d, 69, 82
Plymouth City Museum & Art Gallery	18
Private Collections	1, 3, 23, 24, 26, 29, 40, 45, 51, 56, 64, 66, 71, 77, 78, 81
Robert and Lisa Sainsbury Collection, University of East Anglia	44
Saltwood Castle	7, 67
Mr and Mrs Julian Sofaer	54
Walsall Museum and Art Gallery	4, 63, 79
York City Art Gallery	49

NOTE

Certain foreign terms used in describing drawings have no exact equivalent in English. Among these are **croquis**, which is a brief sketch made from life, usually in a sketchbook; **livre de raison**, a sketchbook used for recording the composition of finished works; **peinture à l'essence**, a technique involving the use of pigment with the oil removed and thinned with turpentine for rapid drying; and **sous-bois**, a forest motif concentrating on vegetation to the exclusion of sky.

Impressionist Drawings

The role of drawing is usually underestimated in the standard literature on Impressionism. The present exhibition takes issue with this evaluation and is intended to show the range of drawings made by Impressionist artists and their associates. It is too easily forgotten that drawings were included, often in substantial numbers, in all eight of the Impressionist exhibitions held between 1874 and 1886, and that they attracted a good deal of attention in reviews.

The selection has been made solely from British collections, both public and private. The search for material has revealed how rich the holdings of Impressionist drawings are in the British Isles. The range extends from the watercolour by Manet (Plate 2) made in connection with the famous painting in the Musée du Louvre, *Le Déjeuner sur l'herbe*, to studies by Seurat (Plates 58, 59) for the equally significant, though totally different, *Dimanche à la Grande-Jatte*, now in The Art Institute, Chicago. Quite apart from these drawings relating to seminal works in European art, there are important sheets by Degas, Pissarro, Renoir and Cézanne. Some artists, notably Mary Cassatt, Gustave Caillebotte and Félix Bracquemond, are not represented simply because drawings could not be located in British collections. However, it is not the purpose of the present exhibition to provide a comprehensive display of the drawing styles of individual artists. Rather, it is to pose fundamental questions about the function of drawing within Impressionism, as opposed to considering stylistic, iconographical and other matters in relation to painting alone. Happily, British collections have provided sheets of good, even outstanding, quality to illustrate the significance of drawing for the Impressionists, and these include a number of items actually shown at their exhibitions.

Questions of definition must obviously be raised. For this exhibition we have concentrated on artists whose work was included in any of the eight Impressionist exhibitions. By this measure, artists like Cézanne and Seurat are referred to as Impressionists. There are also many artists who were closely associated with the Impressionists, but never exhibited with them, and yet others whose styles of painting may not be so readily equated with Impressionism today, but who, none the less, could be acknowledged as such in their own time: Manet and Tissot (Plate 75) are examples of the former category and Gervex (Plate 61) and Duez (Plate 62) of the latter. The organizers felt that little was to be gained by defining Impressionism too narrowly and in this respect the starting-point of the exhibition is that voiced by contemporary critics such as Henry Houssaye, who wrote in *L'Art français depuis dix ans* (Paris, 1882, p. 35): 'Impressionism receives every kind of sarcasm when it takes the names of Manet, Monet, Renoir, Caillebotte, Degas—every honour when it is called Bastien-Lepage, Duez, Gervex . . . Goeneutte . . . or Dagnan-Bouveret.' By about 1880, in fact, the term 'Impressionist' could apply at several levels. It might refer to artists treating modern subjects in a loose, bravura fashion, thus involving a Gervex or a Besnard. In a more specifically Naturalist context, stressing the observation of a moment in contemporary life by means of such technical devices as cursive handling and apparently casual composition, it could incorporate both Degas and Monet. But its most precise definition, with the emphasis on the accurate representation of atmospheric and climatic effects on outdoor motifs, covered only landscape painters like Monet, Sisley and Pissarro. We have, therefore, tried to respect the diverse definitions of Impressionism current a century ago.

Similarly, the word 'drawing' has been broadly defined to incorporate a wide range of media and a great variety of scale. Thus, in terms of media, works executed in pencil, chalk, charcoal, pastel and watercolour have been included, sometimes applied on coloured papers or on other surfaces of differing textures, and often, from the late 1870s, in a mixed form. It will also be apparent how the size and character of the selected drawings differ, extending from *croquis* recorded in an artist's sketchbook to highly finished sheets intended for exhibition and sale. How all these aspects relate to the concept of drawing in Impressionism is the subject of the introductory essays.

This is not a subject that has so far been much discussed and the arguments advanced here are intended to propose a framework for further investigation. While it is undoubtedly true that certain Impressionist painters—Degas, Pissarro, Cézanne—drew regularly throughout their working lives, others, like Monet and Sisley, were less consistent.

Renoir, it seems, drew only intermittently, but at various stages of his life he drew with great intensity, whilst Manet appears to have had a totally functional approach to drawing. Each of these artists, therefore, had different attitudes to the art of drawing. What emerges from an overall examination of the material is the assortment of styles and the wide range of purposes which drawings served. Above all, what is most apparent is the degree to which a dependence on drawing formed part of the Impressionist aesthetic.

CHRISTOPHER LLOYD
RICHARD THOMSON
October 1985

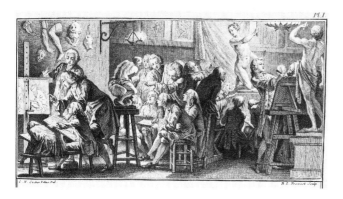

1 Benoit Louis Prévost, after Charles Nicolas Cochin *fils, Vignette from Plate I of the Illustrations for the entry on 'Dessein' in the Encyclopédie,* Vol. IV, Paris, 1754, etching, 10.2 × 20.2 cm. Oxford, Department of the History of Art.

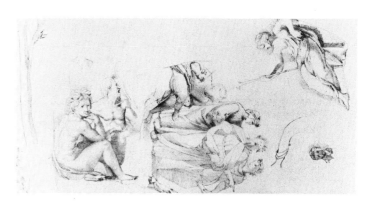

2 Edgar Degas, *Studies after Raphael and Marcantonio Raimondi, c.*1853–6, pen and ink, 15.4 × 31.7 cm. Fogg Art Museum, Cambridge, Mass.

The Academic Tradition and the Emergence of Impressionism

The foundation of the Académie des Beaux-Arts in France in 1648 gave drawing an unimpeachable status. One of the founders, the painter Charles Lebrun, said that drawing was 'the Pole and the compass that guide us', an attitude that persisted well into the nineteenth century.[1] Before the seventeenth century drawing in most European countries had remained a subsidiary, although vitally necessary, part of the creative process, but during that century France, following the example of Italy, made drawing the very basis of art. The practice of drawing was seen not only to develop technical skills of hand and eye, but also to discipline the artist and to ensure that the correct inspirational sources, specifically the Antique and the High Renaissance, were consulted. Drawing, therefore, required both manual and intellectual qualities that were regarded during the seventeenth and eighteenth centuries as the hallmark of the successful artist (Fig. 1). These principles were still being upheld by the ageing Ingres in the mid-nineteenth century when he wrote in defence of the academic system: '. . . drawing is everything, the whole of art lies there. The material processes of painting are very easy and can be learnt in a week or so'.[2]

A rigorous curriculum was introduced for the instruction of drawing at the Académie. The student began by copying prints (Fig. 2) and plaster casts of parts of the body concentrating upon outline (*dessin au trait*) and shading (*dessin ombré*) either by cross-hatching or with stump (*éstompe*). The next stage involved making copies of casts after the Antique (Fig. 3) and then life drawings of posed models (Fig. 4) in which the emphasis was placed upon seeing the form

as a whole. Only when these stages had been mastered was the student encouraged to consider compositional aspects by making copies of finished works in museums and using a sketchbook to record observations made from nature. The emphasis in this training was very much upon the inculcation of a strict discipline based upon a firm sense of tradition; but it contained a major limitation, namely that it taught students to see nature in only one way. The system developed superior drawing technique, but it did not promote spontaneous expression. Similarly, the limitation of media to pencil, chalk and stump hindered freedom of observation. In short, 'the Academy encouraged concentration on the reproduction of an object rather than on its pictorial possibilities'.[3]

During the course of the nineteenth century, however, the authority of the Académie was increasingly challenged. The rapidly changing political situation contributed, by mid-century, to a struggle between entrenched official institutions and an Imperial regime eager to establish a liberal outlook. This clash culminated in the vitally important Decree of November 1863, by which the regime sought to curb the monopolistic control over art previously exercised by the Académie.[4] By appearing to pursue a liberal policy, the government of the Second Empire hoped to harness moderately progressive art to its own propagandist ends. Yet, it was not simply a question of politics. Concomitant with the concern for new social and political ideals in nineteenth-century France was the emergence of an innovative aesthetic based upon the promotion of individual styles resulting from the direct observation of nature and less restricted techniques.

9

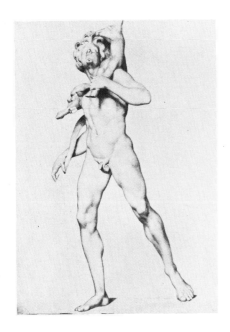

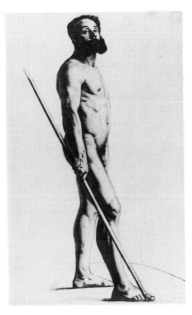

Symbolic of this fusion between politics and art, and also symptomatic of government policy, was the first Salon des Refusés, held in 1863. Its purpose was to accommodate those artists whose work had been rejected by the jury organizing the official Salon. Manet's *Le Déjeuner sur l'herbe* (Fig. 22) was amongst those paintings exhibited at the Salon des Refusés of 1863 and so quite dramatically the 'public was presented with an alternative repertoire to the moribund classic and romantic tendencies sanctioned by academic and most official spokesmen'.[5] Gradually, therefore, alternative styles of painting to that advocated by the Académie were established in France and one of these was Impressionism. By allowing the Salon des Refusés to take place the Government had in fact unintentionally provided a platform for the avant-garde.

The Decree of 1863 also directly affected the teaching of drawing in France in as much as it led to the reform of the École des Beaux-Arts, where several of the future Impressionists—Degas, Pissarro, Seurat—received their initial training.[6] The unreformed École was literally an appendage of the Académie: it was a place where students could improve their skills under the supervision of established masters, many of whom ran their own private studios. Admission to the École was by examination, but the Decree of 1863 extended the facilities to allow promising, but unqualified, students to attend, as well as foreign students. Where previously the École had officially only provided limited instruction in the art of drawing (mainly anatomy and perspective), after the Decree new techniques and new procedures were acknowledged. Many of the early drawings, therefore, by the future Impressionists follow the exacting prescriptions of the long-established academic tradition, but also reveal a slackening in the grip of that same tradition resulting in part from the reforms of 1863. The early drawing by Degas (Plate 20) after Mantegna's painting *Pallas*

Expelling the Vices (Paris, Musée du Louvre, c.1497), most probably dates from c.1855, when the artist was attending the École (Fig. 5). The use of pencil, the clear contours, the web of closely hatched lines, is the basic formula of the academic style, derived from the copying of engravings. The copy also demonstrates the extent to which artists like Degas and others of his generation such as Puvis de Chavannes were attracted just as much by Italian quattrocento painters as by the masters of the High Renaissance favoured by the Académie. Cézanne, who studied at the École des Beaux-Arts at Aix-en-Provence before going to Paris, constantly had recourse to works by older masters either directly or else through reproductions. The copy (Plate 27) after the famous drawing by Signorelli (Fig. 6) in the Musée du Louvre (Cabinet des Dessins), which depicts a man seen from the back carrying a lifeless body, stresses the extent to which Cézanne rapidly moved on from the practice of exact imitation.[7] The smooth modelling and delicate system of highlighting employed by Signorelli has not interested Cézanne, who accents the outlines, reduces the modelling to a minimum and prefers to depict the musculature by linear means. The figure in the copy becomes more dynamic: it is wiry and tensile, more ungainly but truer to life, and clearly related in type to Cézanne's later compositions of bathers (Fig. 7). At the same time Cézanne was looking carefully at Delacroix, from whom he derived the inspiration for some of his early so-called 'romantic' compositions in his 'baroque' style.[8] A sheet by Cézanne in the British Museum (Plate 25) records two mural compositions by Delacroix that were available for inspection in Paris, but were also reproduced in such popular journals as *L'Artiste* and *L'Illustration*, and it is to these that Cézanne most probably made reference in this particular instance (Figs. 8 and 9).[9] He employs open, flowing contours and sudden bursts of hatching to suggest the exuberance of Delacroix's composition

10

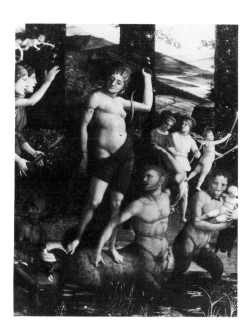 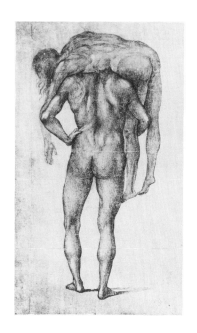 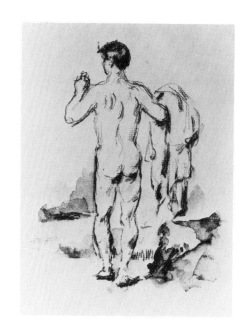

and the dynamism of his brushwork. Quite apart from the stylistic significance of the sheet for Cézanne's personal development, it also demonstrates one of the most remarkable features of artistic life in France during the middle decades of the nineteenth century, a period when numerous reproductions of works of art by recognized masters were being published in the popular press. Copying in front of the masterpieces hanging in the Grande Galerie of the Musée du Louvre was no longer the prerequisite of the favoured student. A spirit of cultural laissez-faire was abroad, and aspiring artists like Manet or Cézanne were free to pillage and ransack tradition at will. Carefully pondered and intricately executed copies after works of art began to give way to hastily observed and rapidly sketched notations.

Training in the academic tradition offered guidance in the choice of subject matter and methods of composition only at a later stage. Degas made several attempts at the start of his career to paint a conventional work depicting a literary or historical scene in the manner of his idol Ingres, whose compositional drawings he later collected (Fig. 10). A whole series of studies exists relating to Degas's early painting *St John the Baptist and the Angel* (1856–8). These are executed in the traditional medium of pencil and examine the poses, movements and drapery of the two protagonists (Plate 19), exploring different elements in the genesis of a history painting.[10] The emphasis in Degas's preparatory methods may have changed over the years, but the constant refining of details remained a feature of the artist's compositional practice (e.g. Plates 33, 34). Similarly, it is indicative of the pervasive influence of the École that Seurat, who enrolled as a student there in 1878, continued, even as an independent artist some three years later, to pose a model in his own studio in the manner of those in the École and to draw her in an almost fully developed tenebrist style (Plate 39).

Study at the École could, however, be supplemented by attendance at one or other of the private studios that proliferated in Paris during the nineteenth century. These were traditionally organized by the leading artists of the day and were often very crowded. The influence of the studio of Ingres, for example, reached almost mythical proportions.[11] By mid-century it was the studios of Thomas Couture and Charles Gleyre that were the best attended. Manet spent six years (1850–6) in Couture's studio where, apart from important technical aspects of painting he may also have derived his drawing style, with its insistent contours, simplified modelling, sense of rounded forms, and preference for softer media (Plates 17, 32, 43).[12] Monet, Bazille, Sisley and Renoir all attended the studio of Gleyre at the beginning of the 1860s, but this common inheritance is perhaps more apparent on a thematic basis than a stylistic one, although there is a possible early influence in the treatment of light by these artists.[13] Alongside the studios headed by famous names, there were more informal and less splendid ateliers that provided further facilities and teaching at comparatively little cost and in a distinctly freer atmosphere. These too were originally formed to provide supplementary teaching for those students who wanted to gain admittance to official institutions, but, in effect, they were places where models were more readily available and posed in a less orthodox manner. It was in these ateliers that new ideas about drawing could be tested. The most famous was perhaps the Académie Julian founded by Rodolphe Julian in 1868, which survived into the present century. It was in fact founded too late to have influenced the Impressionists, although it was influential in the formation of the Nabis and the Fauves and was much frequented by foreign students.[14] Less esteemed, but none the less more important for the Impressionists, was the Académie Suisse, where Pissarro met Monet, Cézanne and Guillaumin at the

11

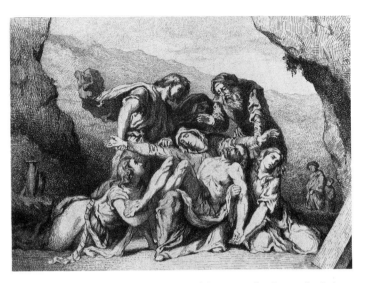

8 Eugène Delacroix, *The Entombment*, wood engraving after the mural painting in the church of St Denis-du-Saint-Sacrement, Paris, published in *L'Artiste*, 2 February 1845, p. 80, 16 × 21.5 cm. British Library, London.

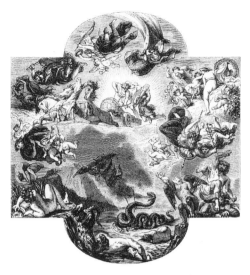

9 Eugène Delacroix, *Apollo Vanquishing the Serpent Python*, wood engraving after the fresco in the Galerie d'Apollon, Palais du Louvre (see *L'Illustration*, 27 December 1851, p. 408), 11.6 × 10.9 cm. Victoria and Albert Museum Library, London.

beginning of the 1860s. The Atelier Suisse was located on the Île de la Cité and it was run by a former model known as Père Suisse. 'There were, properly speaking, neither professors nor pupils. Anyone who wanted to could enrol by paying a fixed sum per month for the model and expenses of upkeep. Everyone worked as he pleased, in pastel, watercolour, oils, copying the model or [working on] some invention of his own, still life or composition; there was complete freedom of experimentation and method.'[15] The more dramatic poses of the models, matched by the bolder treatment made possible by the use of charcoal (in Pissarro's case often applied on blue paper), indicate that several male nude studies by Pissarro and Cézanne (Plates 18, 28) were probably undertaken at the Académie Suisse. A comparison of two sheets by these artists reveals basic differences in their styles. The figures in both studies are prescribed by carefully drawn outlines containing areas of hatching heightened with white. Where Pissarro gently builds up the corpulence of the model's body with carefully gradated shading, Cézanne snatches at the rhythmical contours and impatiently fills in the shadows.

It was not, however, only the institutions that taught drawing, but also basic attitudes to drawing itself that were being freshly examined in France at this time. One of the main controversies arising out of the Decree of 1863 was the debate between Ludovic Vitet, a die-hard conservative, and Viollet-le-Duc, one of the authors of the Decree, concerning teaching methods at the Académie.[16] According to Viollet-le-Duc, the Académie, in its insistence on copying and life-drawing, hampered the development of artistic imagination: 'if, in short, studying the nude is one means, one of the best means, of learning how to draw, it must nevertheless be agreed that copying a nude model wearily holding a pose in an enclosed space and in unchanging lighting conditions is a far cry from producing a picture.'[17] Beyond the confines of 'la salle

d'académie' and traditional sources, he declared, there is '. . . a real sun, real trees, real mountains and real men, going about their business and not posing for the artist'.[18] The same writer had made this point more poetically a year before in an article published in the *Gazette des Beaux-Arts*: 'I am foolish enough to think that a painting lesson, or if one prefers a chat in the park at Saint-Cloud or in the woods at Marly, on a lovely autumn evening, is worth ten of these cold teaching sessions in the studio or the Académie'.[19] For Viollet-le-Duc, therefore, drawing was not a mechanical exercise, but a conscious act of selection from nature matched by a facility of hand. To achieve this he advised teachers of drawing: 'to develop the pupil's powers of observation, to open up his mind to the ever-changing spectacle of nature, to get him to analyse the appearances it presents, to break down the ensembles it offers and to study their details separately, but at the same time to emphasize their relative positions and value. To ensure that, through practice, drawing becomes a constant means of translating the pupil's thoughts or impressions, just as words or the pen become for the orator or writer'.[20]

Viollet-le-Duc's arguments were not developed in a vacuum. He was an eloquent and persuasive spokesman for a body of advanced opinion that had been steadily growing in France. He articulated the spreading disaffection with the Académie and championed new ideas. One of these in particular is of especial interest in the context of Impressionism. This was the method of drawing advocated by Horace Lecoq de Boisbaudran (1802–97), who began as a Salon painter, but in 1841 joined the staff of the École Royale et Spéciale de Dessin, becoming head of the school for three years in 1866.[21] Of his written works the most important is that entitled *L'Education de la mémoire pittoresque*, which was first published in 1848 and reissued in 1862.[22] This publication emphasizes that part of Lecoq's teaching methods concerned with

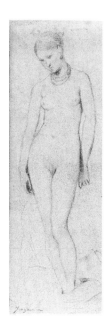

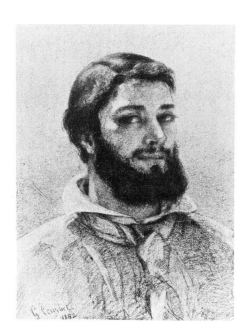

10 Jean Auguste Dominique Ingres, *Standing Female Nude*, c.1820 or mid-1830s, pencil, 24.1 × 8 cm. (Once owned by Degas.) Ashmolean Museum, Oxford.

11 Gustave Courbet, *Self-Portrait*, 1852, charcoal, 56.5 × 45.1 cm. British Museum, London.

drawing from memory. His theory was that students should be encouraged to analyse forms carefully and commit them to memory. It was believed that in this way the constituent elements of a subject could be reproduced more positively and truthfully. Under Lecoq's tuition life-drawing changed completely: models were posed more naturally and many life-classes were conducted in the open air. The drawing by Lhermitte, *Peasant Women Seated in a Church* (Plate 38) possibly dating from 1867, is one of several surviving examples of memory drawings by one of its finest exponents. Often such drawings were done after famous paintings,[23] but Lecoq also insisted, as in the present example, on the artist memorizing scenes from everyday life. Here Lhermitte has memorized the poses, dress and individual features of each figure, but it is because the drawing has been done from memory that it is not overwhelmed by unnecessary detail. The technique required to carry out memory drawings and the situations (both urban and rural) in which Lecoq placed his students encouraged the development of individual artistic talent. Powers of observation were accordingly equated with a fertile artistic imagination. Lecoq's system was adopted by many important

artists, including Fantin-Latour, Legros, Cazin, Lhermitte and Rodin, but it is also apparent that Manet, Degas and Pissarro were not unaffected by it.[24]

Lecoq's theories about drawing were undoubtedly influential, but they were not intended to replace existing practices as exemplified by the École des Beaux-Arts. Rather, he claimed, they were meant to build upon its foundations. 'The École des Beaux-Arts has made it its mission to preserve and hand down the fine traditions of antiquity and the great masters . . . But it forgot that the great masters, whose example it was continually quoting, were not satisfied merely to accept tradition as handed down to them by their predecessors, but sought to combine it with the living elements of their own age, and thus became creators in their turn.'[25] These words describe exactly the position of the Impressionists during the early 1860s when the movement was beginning to establish its own identity. What is of particular significance from an art historical point of view is that contemporary discussions about the art of drawing should have been so closely related to the evolution of Impressionism.

CHRISTOPHER LLOYD

The Impact of Impressionism

The first Impressionist exhibition took place in the spring of 1874, and critical reaction was varied.[26] To a certain extent, some of the initial responses hardened into accepted fact, although to read the main contemporary reviews of the exhibition is to be surprised by the wide range of opinion.[27] The principal criticisms can be assessed under two headings: subject matter and style. For most critics the emphasis of the

exhibition seemed to be on landscape. Ernest Chesneau writing in *Paris-Journal* referred to the painters as 'l'école du plein air', but he also noted in the work of Renoir and Degas a willingness to undertake new subjects: 'Theatre, that aspect of modern life which has until now been completely overlooked in painting, is clearly an obsession with this new school.'[28] What was questioned by several other

13

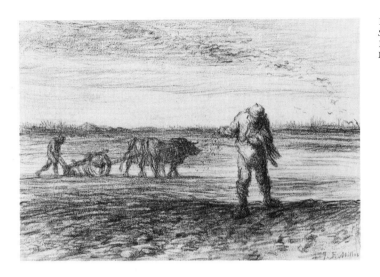

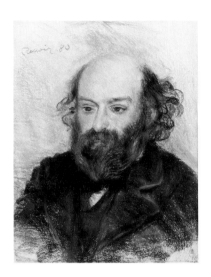

12 Jean-François Millet, *The Sower*, 1850–1, black chalk, 14.6 × 21.2 cm. Ashmolean Museum, Oxford.

13 Auguste Renoir, *Portrait of Cézanne*, 1880, pastel, 53.5 × 44.4 cm. Private Collection.

critics, however, was the suitability of such subject matter for painting.

The style of Impressionist paintings was also seen to be breaking all the conventions: incomplete compositions, loose brushwork, sharp contrasts of light and uncompromising use of colour were features that were difficult to reconcile with Salon paintings. Traditional concepts of balance and harmony of composition were as absent from the paintings of Monet, Pissarro, Cézanne, Degas and Renoir as the sophisticated technique and elevating themes so eagerly desired by the Académie.

Given the somewhat erratic quality of the critical reception of Impressionism, it is hardly surprising that the drawings included in the early exhibitions should have been overlooked. The artistic training received by the Impressionists, the number of surviving drawings and the fact that many were formally exhibited indicates that the art of drawing was by no means alien to Impressionism. Contrary to the widely held belief that the Impressionists painted spontaneously, directly on to the canvas without any preparation, drawing, together with colour, remained the firm basis of their art. Admittedly, each artist had an independent approach to drawing governed not so much by stylistic considerations as by subject—Manet and Degas were concerned principally with urban subjects, Pissarro and Sisley with landscape. Yet, regardless of these distinctions, which were apparent from the first and were to become more pronounced towards the end of the 1870s, drawing does provide a common factor within Impressionism from the outset. In fact the Impressionists, in common with earlier artists, found that it was in drawings that their initial responses (*sensations*) to a motif were best recorded. The traditional use of drawing as a preparatory process remained necessary for transmitting those vitally important momentary sensations experienced *sur le motif* into a compositional context in such a way that

they were rekindled on the canvas. The facture of an Impressionist painting should therefore in reality be more properly described as a simulated spontaneity. What is more, as will be seen, it is a simulation often dependent upon drawing.

The significance of drawing for the Impressionists also has to be understood in relation to the stylistic developments within the movement itself. Jules Castagnary, who was one of the more perceptive critics to attend the first Impressionist exhibition, argued that the movement would be short lived because ultimately it would split into factions.[29] Castagnary may have underestimated the real significance of Impressionism in his review, but he did, none the less, correctly anticipate the division between figure painters and landscape painters that was directly related to the evolution of individual styles and was exacerbated by the desire, or need, for commercial success.[30] The introduction of new exhibitors into the group in an effort to strike a balance between landscape painters like Monet and figure painters like Degas only increased such tensions.[31] Stylistic shifts within Impressionism were becoming evident during the mid-1870s and culminated in the fourth Impressionist exhibition of 1879.[32] Even a cursory inspection shows that paintings executed by Renoir and Monet in 1874 differ considerably in style and technique from those done say two years later. Such rapid changes in style suggest that artists were, on the whole, still prepared at this stage to resolve their problems on the surfaces of their paintings. Degas and Pissarro, on the other hand, maintained their interest in drawing, using it as a means of testing out new ideas. Significantly, it was Degas's example that Edmond Duranty upheld in *La Nouvelle Peinture* (1876), where the role of drawing in Impressionism is emphasized. 'The pencil will be steeped in the very sap of life . . . But drawing is such an individual and indispensable means that we cannot expect from it methods, procedures, or views, it

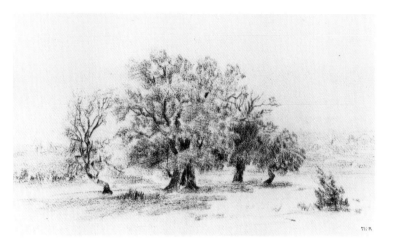

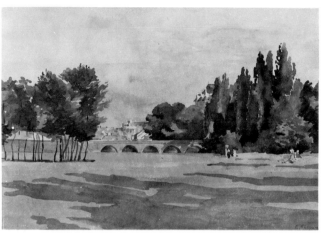

14 Théodore Rousseau, *Groupe de chênes dans les Gorges d'Apremont*, 1850–5, black chalk, 16.8 × 28.4 cm. British Museum, London.

15 Camille Pissarro, *Riverscape near a Town*, c.1865, watercolour, 37 × 54 cm. Nat Loeb Collection, Paris.

merges absolutely with the artist's aim, and is inseparably wedded to the idea.'[33] For Duranty drawing was the primary vehicle for the transcription of modernity and as such was a principal component of Impressionism. For the first time in the history of art, so it would seem, the aesthetics of painting and of drawing began to overlap. This new and significant development, allied to the use of broader techniques, such as coloured chalks and pastel, meant that the old arbitrary division between brush and pencil was gradually abandoned: the hierarchy of traditional values was finally eroded. Indeed, in the cases of drawings executed in gouache, tempera or *essence* on such surfaces as linen, canvas or board the method of application was directly with the brush. It is true that some of the essential freedoms in the art of drawing had been established earlier in the century: watercolour was closely linked to the popular topographical tradition; the chalk and charcoal drawings of Courbet (Fig. 11) and particularly of Millet (Fig. 12) had revealed the potential of tonal drawing; and the highly refined portrait drawings of Ingres had raised this genre to a new level.[34] The Impressionists, however, were to develop all these aspects of drawing. The fact that certain media were no longer so dogmatically associated with specific types of drawing presented the artists with a freedom of choice that paralleled the dexterity of their brushwork, just as it matched the contemporaneity of their subject matter. It is the reciprocity between subject matter and medium that established drawing in the context of Impressionism alongside painting and print-making as a vital means of recording fugitive effects. The inclusion of drawings and prints in the Impressionist exhibitions invested the graphic arts with a significance that the official Salon had so far failed to recognize and thus gave drawing a new and controversial status.[35]

An analysis of the main categories of drawings dating from the 1870s and slightly before will illustrate the main aspects of Impressionist drawing at this stage of its evolution. Portraits dating from the 1870s evoke comparison with works by eighteenth-century masters such as Quentin de la Tour, Chardin, Liotard in their preference for pastel.[36] The smoothly modelled surfaces of earlier pastellists were, however, not emulated, and portraits by the Impressionists in this medium are notable for the uneven balance between the traditional half- or three-quarters length poses and the freedom with which the medium is handled. Renoir in his *Head of a Young Woman with Red Hair* (Plate 68) of c.1876–8 comes closest to such rococo precedents in the handling of pastel, especially in the treatment of the flesh tones. Pissarro, by comparison, in his *Portrait of Marie Daudon* (Plate 15) of 1876 uses pastel in a way that is more closely related to Impressionist painting. There is a sudden shift from the brilliant red of the shawl to the vivid black of the dress and in the face itself the transition from light to shadow on the right gives the visage an almost carved aspect. Towards the end of the 1870s Renoir's pastels were executed in a looser style. The famous *Portrait of Cézanne* (Fig. 13) of 1880 captures the volatility of Cézanne's character by the colour contrast of yellow and black and by framing the head with loose, almost wild, wisps of hair. A similar abundance of black combined with high-toned colours can be found in Renoir's *Head of a Young Woman* (Plate 41) dating from c.1878–80. Where Renoir is effusive in his application of pastel, Manet is restrained. The *Portrait of Marie Colombier* (Plate 40) of c.1880 and the *Portrait of Suzette Lemaire* (Plate 76) reveal the balancing act that the artist performs between broadly worked areas and subtle dabs of colour, between highly finished parts, such as the hair, and roughly indicated passages, such as the shoulders, and between firmly indicated contours and implied line. Manet, like a sculptor, develops these images around a slender armature, relying on the textured surfaces—skin, hair, silk—to

15

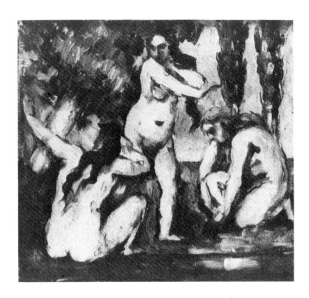

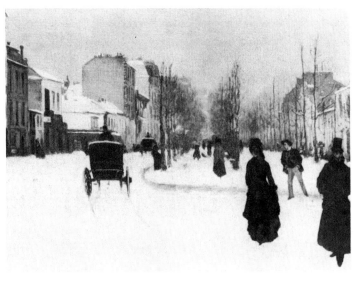

16   Paul Cézanne, *Three Female Bathers*, 1875–7, oil, 22 × 19 cm. Musée d'Orsay (Galeries du Jeu de Paume), Paris.

17   Norbert Goeneutte, *Boulevard de Clichy under Snow*, 1875–6, oil, 60 × 73.5 cm. Tate Gallery, London.

suggest a living presence to the observer.

An even greater variety is found in the landscape or cityscape drawings of the 1870s in which movement, light and atmosphere had to be recorded swiftly while the artist worked *sur le motif* in the open air. Pissarro's early compositional landscape drawing done at Chailly in black chalk *c*.1857 (Plate 22) was directly inspired by artists of the Barbizon School, especially Théodore Rousseau (Fig. 14). The foliage is rendered with small, neat touches gently stroked on to a mid-toned paper. Greater attention is paid to composition in Pissarro's drawing of Nanterre (Plate 21), with the path leading into the wooded background. The vigorous hatching and the accented lines in black chalk highlighted with touches of white on a grey paper not only suggest a restless eye and an energetic hand, but also lend the composition a tautness that is lacking in the drawing of Chailly. Sisley in the mid-1870s, working on the banks of the Seine, achieves a comparable visual charge in applying black chalk to white paper (Plate 70). The landscape is drawn with a host of much looser lines spread across the sheet like iron filings: some are open, long and flowing, while others are short and jagged. The sky is left blank so that the scene is dominated by an intense luminosity. One might almost say that in this drawing Sisley has produced a positive to set alongside Seurat's negative (Plate 58).

The watercolour tradition, so widely practised at the beginning of the nineteenth century, was exploited in a similar way.[37] Topographical accuracy was by no means forgotten, but it came to be expressed differently. The watercolours of artists like Harpignies, Jacquemart and Jongkind (Plate 66), all of whom were influential contemporaries of the Impressionists, combined precision with breadth— the former evident in the detailing of visual data and the latter in the silhouetting of forms accurately placed on the paper with rhythmical, supple brushstrokes. Atmosphere is combined with anecdotal detail, just as

observation is matched by manual dexterity. Also important for the Impressionists was the varying degree of finish found in the watercolour tradition. Early watercolours by Pissarro (Fig. 15) show how conscious he was of mid-nineteenth-century practice, but later in the decade Morisot, who exhibited several watercolours in the first Impressionist exhibition, demonstrated by her spirited brushwork how the desire to provide a mere visual record of a scene had been replaced by the attempt to suggest what it was actually like to be moving through the landscape itself (Plate 5).

It is the brushwork also that is the chief hallmark of Cézanne's watercolour study (Plate 8) for the painting *Three Female Bathers* dating from the mid-1870s, when the artist was working in an Impressionist manner (Fig. 16). The network of blue, green and yellow washes applied with small, fairly even strokes has a freshness and crispness that evokes the cool atmosphere of a sylvan glade where the bathers disport themselves in a composition reminiscent of Titian and Rubens. Of all the Impressionists Cézanne was the one who most sustained his dependence upon watercolour and he included three examples in the third Impressionist exhibition of 1877, the last at which he showed his work.[38] If during the 1860s and 1870s he tended to make watercolours as part of the preparatory process, his attitude to the medium changed during the later decades, when he invested it with an importance which rivalled that of his paintings (Plates 7, 64, 65). The spatial intervals of a still-life subject or of a landscape are captured by the subtle and economical exploitation of the medium. Clear, translucent patches of colour applied deftly, but logically, with a fully loaded brush float around brief indications of outline. The paper on which the image is made is accepted as being a positive part of the drawing: not only does it serve physically as the support, but it also represents light and distance at the same time. What distinguishes

16

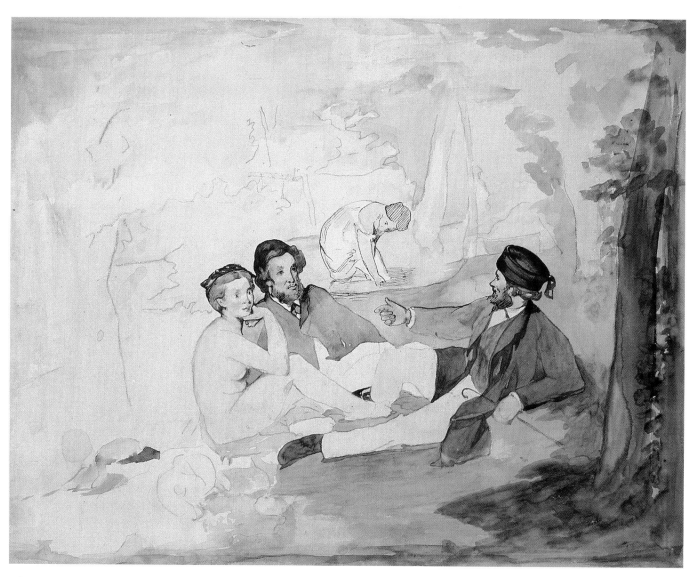

2 Édouard Manet, *Le Déjeuner sur l'herbe*. 1863. Ashmolean Museum, Oxford (Cat. No. 36).

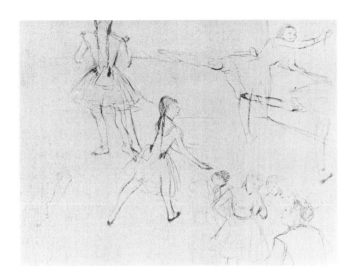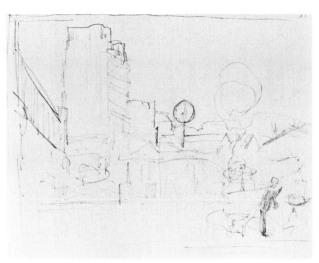

18 Edgar Degas, *Studies of Ballet Dancers Rehearsing* (page 25 from Notebook 28), 1877, pencil, 24.8 × 34 cm. Formerly Collection of Ludovic Halévy, Paris.

19 Claude Monet, *Gare Saint-Lazare, Paris*, 1877, pencil, 24 × 31 cm. Musée Marmottan, Paris.

Cézanne's watercolours, therefore, is the intellectual rigour brought to the composition and the precision of the technique itself.

Even greater advances were made in the use of pastel for landscapes. The pastels of Boudin, a number of which were shown at the first Impressionist exhibition as well as at the Salons, clearly inspired the young Monet. The comparison of marine pastels by these two masters (Plates 14, 16) reveals Boudin's consummate skill in treating the surface of the whole sheet of paper with a series of horizontal strokes applied with different pressures of the hand, which seem to be disposed at random, but coalesce at a distance to form a composition of the type so aptly described by Baudelaire in his review of the Salon of 1859 as 'liquid or aerial enchantments'.[39] Monet, who like Boudin also exhibited pastels at the first Impressionist exhibition, is understandably more nervous of the medium. His composition is more carefully structured, the transition from sea to sky more clearly demarcated even though the strokes of yellow and orange amidst the darkening sea and sky herald a more literal and vigorous rendition of lighting effects. Guillaumin, too, began to use pastel at an early date. The style of *Le Quai de Bercy* (Plate 47) of 1867 is more individual and forceful than Monet's early pastel (Plate 14), but a sense of tradition is still apparent in the carefully unified tones. A similar equivocation can be found in an early pastel by Pissarro, *Apple Picking* (Plate 57) of 1872, where he has used only green pastel in conjunction with black and white chalks on buff-coloured paper. Although liberally applied, the pastel is restricted to a single area regarded partly as local colour and partly as a highlight. On the other hand, Pissarro's pastel of the *Boulevard de Clichy* (Plate 6), dated 1880 but exhibited in the sixth Impressionist exhibition of 1881, reveals a considerable technical advance. He has positioned himself above street-level looking down on the carriages and pedestrians moving in and out of the picture space. The scene is animated with impulsive bursts and splashes of high-toned pastel (yellow, orange, blue, mauve) so that it captures not only the rapidity of movement inherent within this busy street-scene, but also the sharp light of a winter's day. What is particularly imposing is the large scale of this pastel which rivals that of a painting, unlike the pastels of Boudin and Monet. Furthermore, on comparison with the paintings and etchings of the boulevard de Clichy by Norbert Goeneutte (Fig. 17) and Félix Buhot, it can be seen how Pissarro's carefully chosen viewpoint above the street enables him to be less descriptive in style and to concentrate more on atmosphere and light.[40]

It is all too easy to overlook the fact that the compositional procedures adopted by the Impressionists continued to be based on tradition. The stress laid on the *plein-air* principles of Impressionist landscape painting is essentially correct, but a surprising amount of preparatory work was none the less undertaken before a painting was begun. Part of the process was the recording of motifs, or visual data, that could form the basis of a composition or else be incorporated into it. The notebooks of Degas, preserved mainly in the Bibliothèque Nationale, provide ample evidence of a lifetime of intense observation (Fig. 18).[41] Monet, Pissarro, Gauguin and, during the early part of his career, Seurat, also filled sketchbooks with visual *aides-mémoire*. The drawings found in these sketchbooks are *croquis*, best defined as rapid studies made from life. Manet (Plate 45), for example, whose penchant for line lent itself admirably to *croquis*, watches a cripple walking down the street; Degas (Plates 35, 36) waits patiently in rehearsal rooms to observe dancers; Boudin (Plate 16) spies on rows of figures indulging in the pleasures of the sea-shore and animates them with the skill of a puppeteer; Pissarro goes into the fields to chart patterns of labour (Plate 78). All these examples of *croquis* are deftly executed

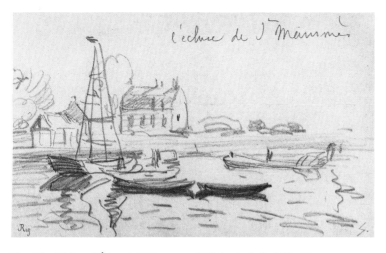

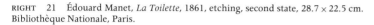

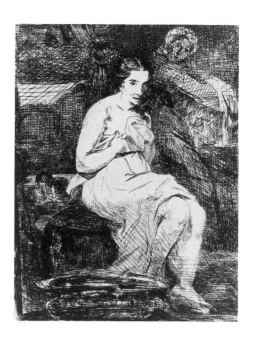

20   Alfred Sisley, *L'Écluse de St Mammès*, c.1885, black chalk, 12.9 × 21 cm. Museum Boymans-van Beuningen, Rotterdam.

RIGHT   21   Édouard Manet, *La Toilette*, 1861, etching, second state, 28.7 × 22.5 cm. Bibliothèque Nationale, Paris.

studies invariably on a small scale and often annotated. Such drawings served as the raw material from which the main subject of a painting, or else merely incidental details, could be derived. Comparison of the four *croquis* mentioned here reveals differences of approach that were to become a central issue in Impressionism by the late 1870s, namely the division between pure landscape painters and figure painters. Manet and Degas worked close up to the subject, studying the pose or a specific movement and making notations on anatomical details or on a possible change in position. As primarily figure painters they sought the particular. Boudin and Pissarro, however, saw the human figure in a wider, more general context. They viewed the subject from a distance, and the notations on their drawings reflect a concern with the effects of light and colour. By contrast, the sketchbooks of Monet and Sisley were rarely filled with *croquis*. Monet made drawings with ebullient gestures of the hand, the fluidity of line serving as a rehearsal for the brush (Fig. 19), whereas Sisley adopted a more oratorial style (Fig. 20). Both artists used their sketchbooks to record fully resolved compositions.[42]

The compositional process developed by the Impressionists was frequently complicated and varied. Even in the early 1860s Manet was especially radical both in his interpretation of subject matter and in his preparatory methods: so much so that there is still considerable debate about both of these issues. For instance, he used the traditional medium of red chalk for a drawing (Plate 32) executed in the reverse direction for the transfer of a design on to a copper plate made ready for etching. The subject is a variant of a painting known as *The Surprised Nymph* (Buenos Aires, Museo Nacional de Bellas Artes) of 1859–61, which was by degrees transformed into the etching entitled *La Toilette* (Fig. 21). Although corresponding to the etching in most respects (indeed, the contours are indented), Manet even at this late stage continues

in the drawing to show uncertainty as to the exact format: the figure could have been either a half-length or a full-length. The problems arising from the watercolour (Plate 2) related to his painting *Le Déjeuner sur l'herbe* of 1863 are even more perplexing because the picture exists in two versions (Figs. 22 and 23), the main one in Paris (Musée du Louvre) that had such a *succès de scandale* at the Salon des Refusés, and the other version, of smaller dimensions, in London (Courtauld Institute Galleries). The watercolour differs in certain respects from both the painted versions and the purpose of the drawing is made even harder to assess because it is not absolutely clear as to which of the painted versions was executed first. It is reasonable to assume, given the size and significance attached by Manet to the composition, that he painted an elaborate oil sketch for it in the traditional manner, and that this can be identified with the painting in London. It was admittedly his custom to make watercolours in connection with etchings after his own paintings, but these are usually more highly finished. The watercolour in question is relatively unfinished and is technically in mixed media: pencil outlines indicate the basic forms while watercolour has been added to some areas and hatched strokes made with pen and dark ink are laid over others. It is therefore difficult to determine exactly whether the exploratory character of the drawing is related to the preparatory work for *Le Déjeuner sur l'herbe* or to Manet's preoccupation with developing the composition further.

Renoir showed a similar sleight of hand in his preparatory processes during the 1870s.[43] A fine and somewhat rare example of a preparatory study (Plate 54) exists for the painting *Two Little Circus Girls* of 1879 (Fig. 24). Interestingly, when Edmond Renoir, the artist's brother, was writing about this picture in *La Vie Moderne* he particularly stressed the spontaneity of the artistic process as being characteristic of Impressionism.[44] Yet the nature of this preparatory

19

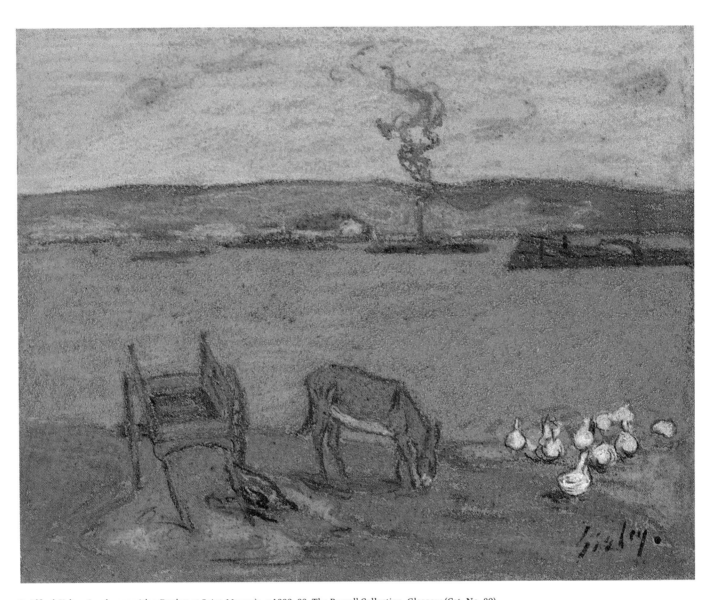

3 Alfred Sisley, *Landscape with a Donkey at Saint-Mammès. c.*1880–90. The Burrell Collection, Glasgow (Cat. No. 80).

4 Edgar Degas, *Portrait of a Seated Woman. c.*1885. Whitworth Art Gallery, University of Manchester (Cat. No. 22).

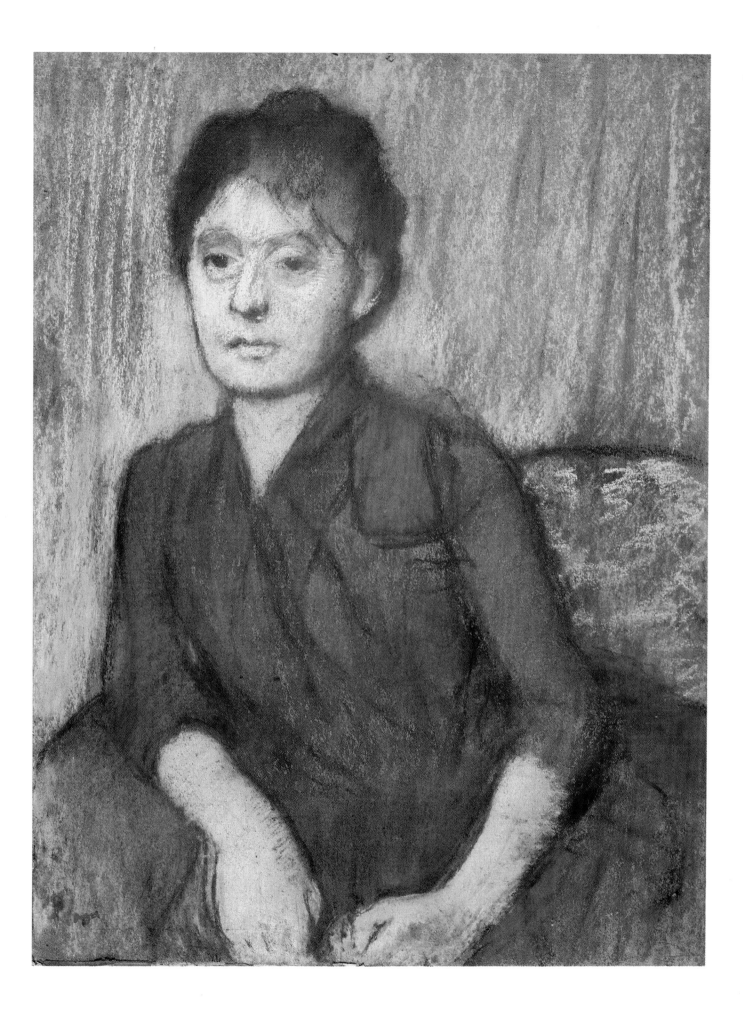

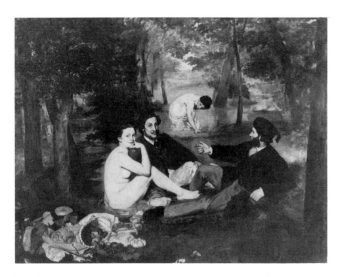

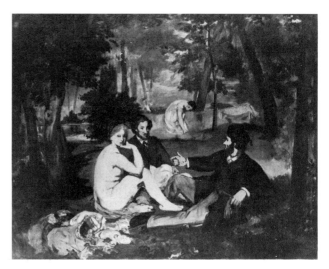

22 Édouard Manet, *Le Déjeuner sur l'herbe*, 1863, oil, 208 × 264 cm. Musée d'Orsay (Galeries du Jeu de Paume), Paris.

23 Édouard Manet, *Le Déjeuner sur l'herbe*, 1862–3, oil, 89.5 × 116.5 cm. Courtauld Institute Galleries, London.

drawing would suggest that there was little that could be described as spontaneous in Renoir's attempt to arrive at the final composition. The drawing included an extra figure of a clown in the lower right corner on a diagonal with the two circus girls, one of whom is placed in the centre and the other at the far left. On rearranging the composition Renoir omitted the clown and extended the space on the left so that the girls are more isolated and dominate the centre together, thus becoming the real subject of the picture. The black chalk has been so delicately applied over the surface of the linen-faced paper that it is as if Renoir is exploring like a blind man the very shape of the figures and discovering their spatial possibilities. Although outlines are evident, the emphasis is on tonal nuance, with accented flicks for the hair, the facial features and the costumes. The significance of this drawing lies in the fact that the spontaneity so often associated with Impressionist painting is in essence a delayed or recaptured spontaneity translated from one medium into another. Drawings serve as the agents of spontaneity, recording observations extracted from a world in a state of flux.

By the close of the 1870s several of the Impressionist painters were concerned to devise more complicated compositions in an attempt to develop their styles more fully. It was principally Degas who both promoted this process and showed the way. He made whole series of drawings demonstrating endless powers of invention in the treatment of single figures: he would test out poses and elaborate them on numerous sheets before deciding whether to incorporate them in a painting or reject them. One of the major ballet pictures by Degas of these years is *The Rehearsal* (Shelburne, Vermont, The Shelburne Museum), which was included in the fourth Impressionist exhibition of 1879, although it was probably executed in 1875–6 (Fig. 25).[45] The painting involved Degas in a number of preparatory studies in different media for almost every figure in the composition. The study for the violinist (Plate 34) appears to have been drawn from life. Degas was apparently well satisfied with this particular pose and squared up the drawing immediately, ready for transfer to the canvas; it is also inscribed like a *croquis* with a notation about the fall of light. The basic principle of this compositional method is additive. Degas is daring in his use of spatial intervals, groups of figures being offset by areas of void, but within the limits of the composition he inserts the figures with great precision. Essentially, however, when the drawings are seen in relation to the finished picture it can be appreciated to what extent *The Rehearsal* is a composite work.

Comparison with a painting by Degas with the same title dating from 1878–9 and now in the Frick Collection, New York, reveals the extent to which he refined his compositional procedure towards the end of the decade (Fig. 26).[46] The later composition has been simplified not only by reducing the number of figures, but also by omitting unnecessary detail—for example, the obliteration of the view through the curtains to a courtyard and the less fussy painting of the diaphanous curtains themselves. The poses of the dancers are unified by concentrating on a single group, as opposed to being contrasted in two separate groups. This concern for a more unified design is again reflected in Degas's use of drawings, so that a single study could be incorporated in several different works, sometimes being repeated without change, sometimes only with minor adjustments (Fig. 27).[47] Degas relied on drawing to an almost unprecedented degree. It not only provided a plentiful supply of poses and motifs, but also served to promote the creative process. Such a method of working, pioneered during the 1870s, was critical for the later stages of Impressionism. If it is true that the Impressionists drew a great deal, it could never be argued that they were profligate in the use they made of their drawings.

CHRISTOPHER LLOYD

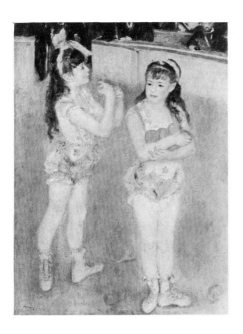

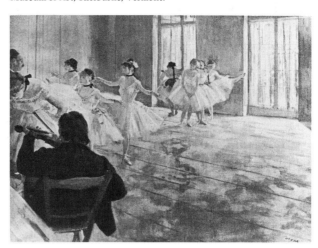

24   Auguste Renoir, *Two Little Circus Girls*, 1879, oil, 130.8 × 98.5 cm. The Art Institute of Chicago (Potter Palmer Collection), Chicago.

25   Edgar Degas, *The Rehearsal*, 1875–6, oil, 43 × 57 cm. Shelburne Museum of Art, Shelburne, Vermont.

Impressionism and Drawing in the 1880s

1879: Drawing into Focus

The function of drawing in Impressionist art during the 1880s is a complex subject. It is a field rich in experiment and variety, and in interrelationships extending beyond the avant-garde community to wider artistic and economic matters. 1879 was a pivotal year, which set the tone for the following decade. In that year all the central protagonists, aesthetic issues and commercial concerns which can be charted during the 1880s came sharply into focus.

At the fourth Impressionist exhibition held that year Degas had the dominant role. He showed an important group of works, varied in subject and in range of media.[48] He also introduced friends to fortify the position of the figure painters within the Impressionist group, thus placing greater emphasis on draughtsmanship. These recruits were Marie Bracquemond, Mary Cassatt, Forain, Gauguin, Lebourg, Somm and Federigo Zandomeneghi. The influence of Degas and the new status of drawing were implicit in the hanging of the exhibition and were recognized by critics. Henry Havard remarked how one room had notable drawings by Henri Rouart, Ludovic Piette, and Lebourg, among them *Reading (Evening)* (Plate 60), with Mme Bracquemond, Forain and Degas in the next. The 'high priests of Impressionism', including Monet and Pissarro, were in the last room.[49] Landscape was by now acknowledged to be a separate subsection of Impressionism.[50] Degas's importance was clearly understood, with stress being put on the experimental quality of his work: 'one

certainly couldn't find a better comparison for these restless researches into new techniques, these mixtures of tempera [*détrempe*] and pastel, these essays in *peinture à l'essence*, these combinations of multi-coloured frames, than experiments in a laboratory.'[51] Cassatt and Forain were considered Degas's pupils, and he had intended to feature yet more figurative artists. One of his notebooks reveals that he planned to include Raffaëlli, who showed the following year, and Lhermitte, a leading Naturalist draughtsman.[52]

The 1879 exhibition displayed a greater proportion of drawings than previous (or later) Impressionist shows: they constituted about one third of the works on view.[53] It would be an oversimplification to grant this initiative to Degas alone, for Pissarro submitted— alongside his twenty-two oil paintings—twelve fans and four pastels, three of them portraits. It was the first time that he had exhibited drawings, and his professional friendship with Degas, then intense, was evidently important. Yet Pissarro had been encouraged to undertake figure subjects in emulation of Millet by the critic Théodore Duret in 1874.[54] To combine the tradition of Millet's rustic figures and Degas's technical and compositional innovations was surely a challenge to Pissarro by 1879, and it was no doubt stimulated too by the success of the sale of Millet pastels from the Gavet collection following the artist's death in 1875. Furthermore, Pissarro had suffered badly in 1878, a poor year generally for Impressionist fortunes on the art market. At the Hoschedé sale in June his paintings had averaged 45 francs,[55] and in the wake of this it was no coincidence that at the 1879

23

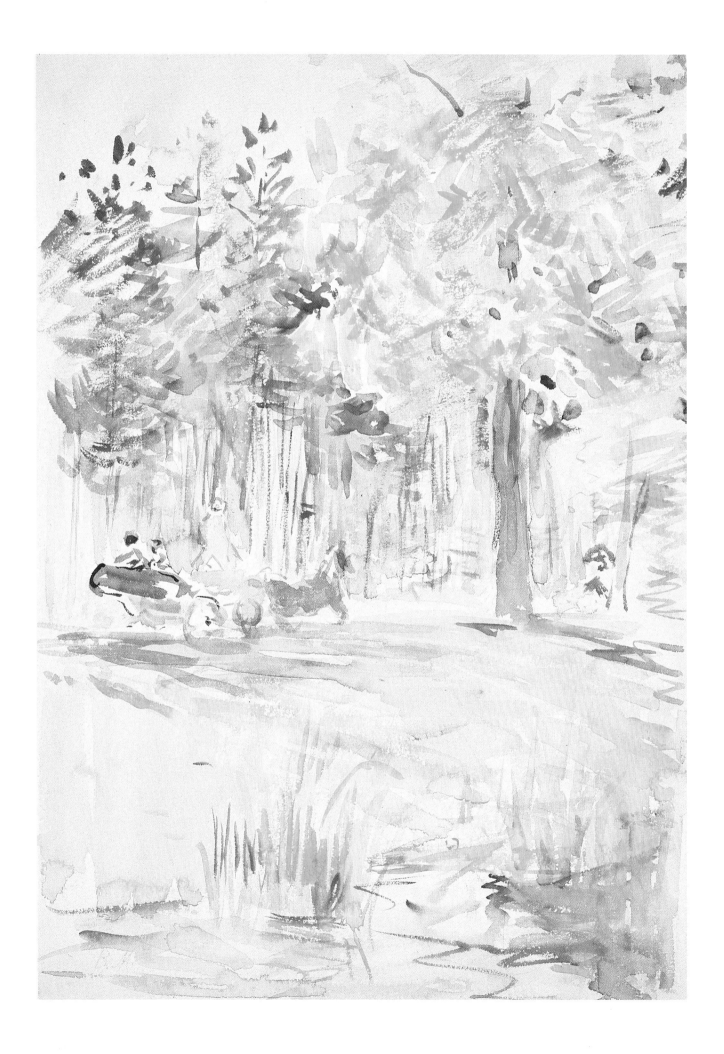

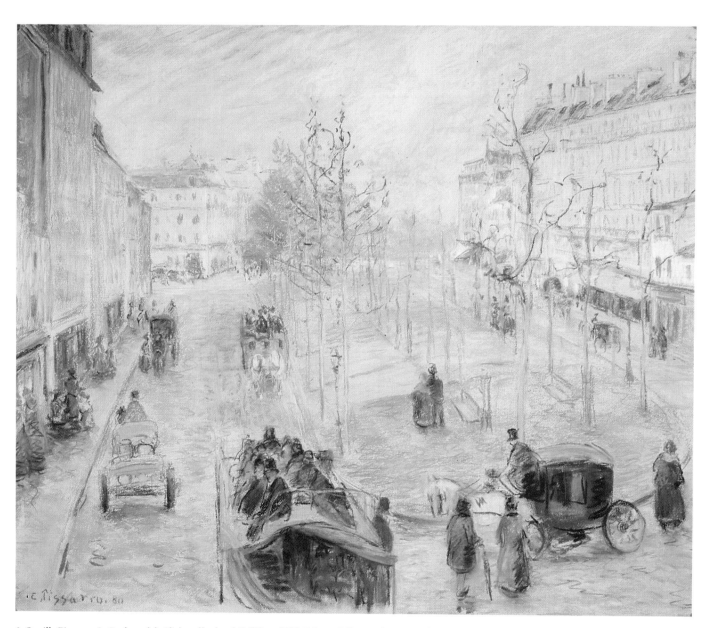

6 Camille Pissarro, *Le Boulevard de Clichy, effet de soleil d'hiver*. 1880. Private Collection (Cat. No. 51).

5 Berthe Morisot, *Carriage in the Bois de Boulogne*. c.1874 or later. Ashmolean Museum, Oxford (Cat. No. 43).

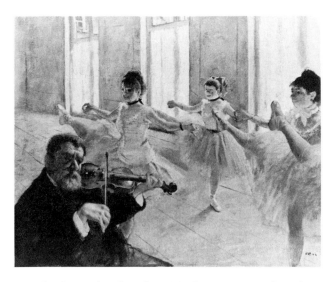

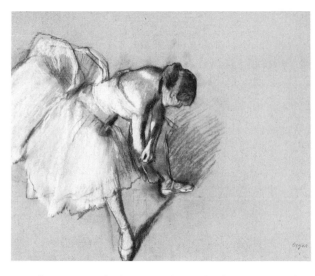

26 Edgar Degas, *The Rehearsal*, 1878–9, oil, 47.6 × 60.9 cm. The Frick Collection, New York.

27 Edgar Degas, *Study of a Dancer Adjusting her Shoe*, c.1880, pastel and charcoal, 49 × 62 cm. Private Collection.

Impressionist exhibition he showed such saleable items as fans and pastel portraits.

Pissarro was not the only artist to experience hardship at this time, and Impressionist drawing in general must be considered within the context of the fragile French economy of the 1880s and of the bourgeois art market. Commercial pressures, for instance, lay behind the foundation of the Société d'Aquarellistes Français in 1879. The motives for forming this group, which included artists as varied as Gustave Doré and the military painter Detaille, were mixed: firstly, to resurrect the standard of French watercolour painting, which had looked weak in comparison with that of the English works shown at the Paris Universal Exhibition of 1878; and secondly to give a delicate medium the chance to flower outside the crowded Salon. It was also suspected that the gambit was engendered by 'some ingenious dealers'.[56] The Société's highly finished work was aimed at the de luxe market; to Degas's friend Diego Martelli, it had the same faults 'as bonbons, [for] it's expensive, takes great patience to create, gives no nourishment, and if abused, ends in terrible indigestion.'[57] Nevertheless, the Aquarellistes' activity reflects the burgeoning middle-class market for works other than oils and the dealer system devised to exploit it. It was a market in which the Impressionist artists had to win a place.

Another element vital to Impressionist draughtsmanship came to the fore in 1879. By this time advances in printing technology had greatly facilitated the mechanical reproduction of images in books and magazines. 1879 saw the much-welcomed commencement of regular publication of *Le Salon Illustré*, with major works from the annual Salon reproduced by the artists' own drawings.[58] There was also the foundation of the illustrated weekly *La Vie Moderne*, which with its accompanying gallery was sympathetic to the Impressionists. So with the possibility of their work becoming known to a wider public not through

the intermediary of a reproductive print but by an illustration of their own drawing, artists could gain publicity in a particularly advantageous fashion.

Indeed, in the 1880s drawings generally became objects of considerable interest in France. The collections and bequests of old master drawings of collectors such as His de la Salle were aired in art historical publications. A superb facsimile edition of the Louvre's finest old master sheets was published in 1882; it was now possible to take home great drawings, enthused one critic, 'like mineral water'.[59] An exhibition of *Les Dessins du Siècle*, from David and Prud'hon to contemporaries such as Puvis de Chavannes and Lhermitte, was held at the École des Beaux-Arts in 1884 to wide acclaim.[60] The old prejudices against drawing—that it was a lesser artform than painting, that preparatory work should be kept clandestine—were increasingly criticized. One writer in 1884, for instance, demanded more space for drawings in the Salon and the purchase by the State of preparatory studies alongside finished work.[61]

Drawing as Synthesis

During the 1880s an increasing number of artists in the Impressionist circle came both to recognize and to employ drawing as a more crucial element in their work. This was not merely an issue of everyday practice, but also of intellectual purpose, for drawing became a means whereby crucial stylistic problems were raised and solved. Drawing's value was two-fold, rich and complex in its cross-fertilization. Working on paper gave the artist the opportunity to visualize and think through pictorial problems in a more direct manner than the potentially intractable medium of oil paint. Yet at the same time, the Impressionists' avoidance of pencil—the graphic tool most divorced from painting—and their preference for media such as

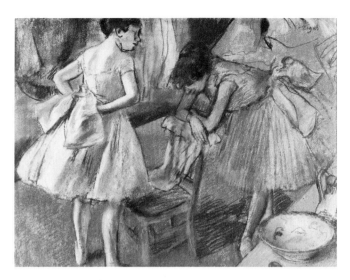

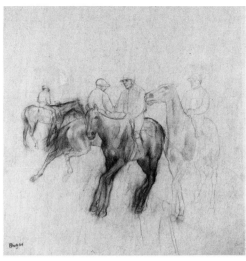

28   Edgar Degas, *Two Dancers in their Dressing Room*, *c*.1880, pastel on buff paper, 48.5 × 64 cm. National Gallery of Art, Dublin.

29   Edgar Degas, *Group of Jockeys*, *c*.1868, pencil on brown paper, 49 × 42 cm. Collection of Mr and Mrs Eugene Victor Thaw, New York.

pastel, tempera and sanguine ensured that their drawings were intimately related, in colour and texture as well as in compositional and formal concerns, to the matter of painting. Within the broad Impressionist group different aims co-existed—those of Degas were far from Monet's—and it is of help to separate figure subjects from landscape. This distinction was made by contemporaries, and implicitly recognizes drawing as the traditional medium for exploring the figure as well as the predominance of oil paint in France as the prime medium for landscape. What co-ordinates the varying initiatives within Impressionism at this period was the search, both conceptual and stylistic, for a refined pictorial unity, for synthesis. By the last Impressionist exhibition in 1886 critics like Paul Adam acclaimed the harmonious, decorative distillation of observed reality.[62] What part did drawing play in this achievement?

For Degas drawing was an intellectual rather than an instinctive activity. In his preparation for paintings such as *The Rehearsal* in the 1870s (Fig. 25)—a process based on organizing autonomous figures first realized on paper into a coherently composed ensemble—he conceived drawing as the articulation of form, and design as the manipulation of space. These were distinct, if overlapping functions in the evolution of a multi-figure composition. Annotations made in a notebook *c*.1880 bear witness to his pragmatic, organizational attitude to drawing: 'Projects for the studio / put up steps around the room / to accustom myself to draw things from above and below / only paint things seen in a mirror to encourage hatred of *trompe l'œil* / have a portrait posed on the ground floor / and work on the second, to get used to / memorizing forms and expressions and to never / drawing or painting immediately.'[63] A drawing like *Two Dancers in their Dressing Room* (Fig. 28) can be seen almost as a product of the first admonition; it is as if Degas stood on their dressing-table to draw. Yet often, as here, he chose an unusual viewpoint to enliven otherwise banal poses—how symmetrical the left-hand dancer would have been if seen head on. In *Two Dancers* Degas concerned himself with ambient light, adapting his handling accordingly; the patches of bare paper and the smudged pastel on the left figure and the tighter hatching on the right correspond to the fall of light. Above all, he avoided unobtrusive accessories, using contour to orchestrate the composition's main rhythms rather than to describe a single static form. This trend of leading from the particular to the general had been a central current in Degas's work for some time before 1880. *Jockeys in the Rain* (Plate 12), for example, had its origins in a small race-course painting of the late 1860s, a scrupulously prepared genre scene including spectators which are just visible in one of his preliminary drawings (Fig. 29). Via a painting exhibited at the 1879 Impressionist exhibition, this composition culminated some fifteen years later in *Jockeys in the Rain*.[64] Detail and genre elements were discarded. A subtle composition remains, at once disjointed and articulate. The tart warms and cools of the jockey's colours act as accents against the enveloping tones of the landscape, and the wedge of horses is both a broken frieze and a satisfying sequence of movement. Degas's refinement of motifs, the increasingly synthetic simplification of his drawing, and his awareness of unifying atmosphere set a remarkable example for other artists in the early 1880s.

When, from the end of the 1870s, Pissarro began to concentrate more on the figure, it was to Degas's example that he largely turned. This is apparent in *The Harvest* (Fig. 31), a major tempera painting shown at the Impressionist exhibition of 1882. Pissarro started with ideas for the whole composition, first making a wash drawing on squared paper (Fig. 30) and then a pastel, both from imagination.[65] Next he specified certain figures, some of which had their origins in *croquis* (Plate 78). The magnificent sheet in Oxford

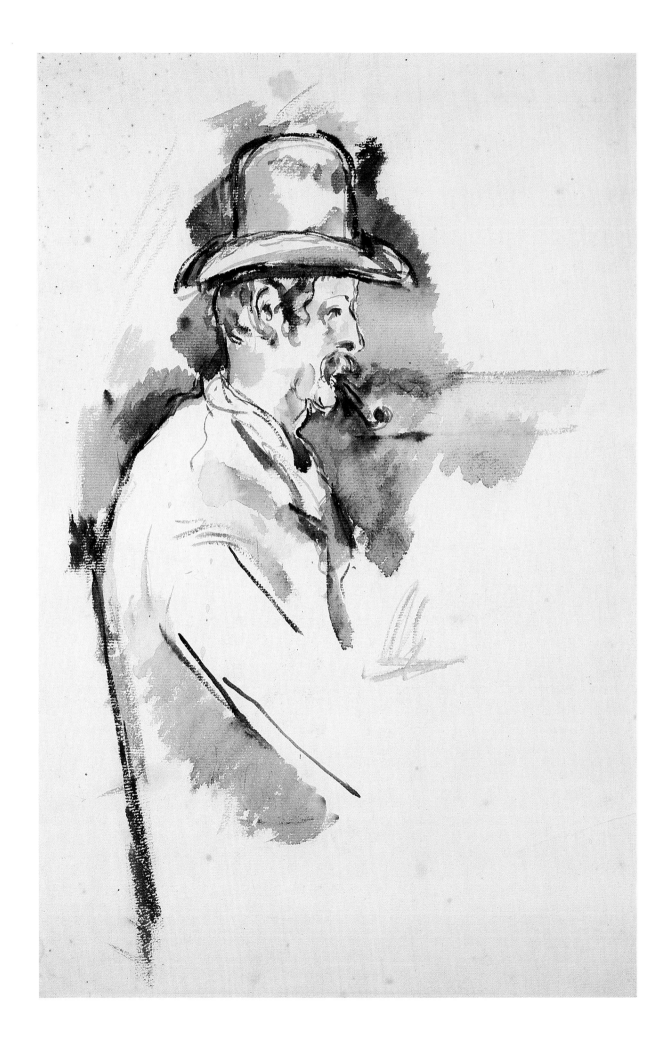

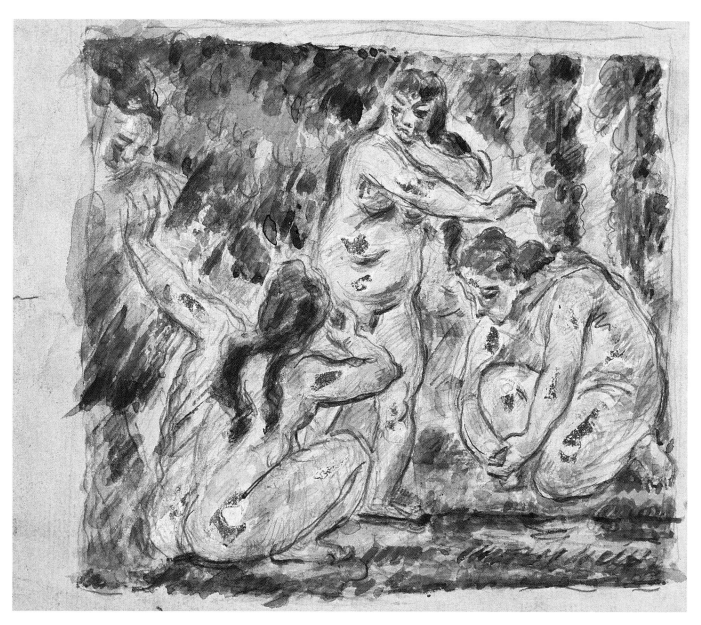

8 Paul Cézanne, *Three Female Bathers*. 1874–5. National Museum of Wales, Cardiff (Cat. No. 8).

7 Paul Cézanne, *L'Homme à la pipe*. 1892–6. Lent by Thomas Gibson Fine Art—Agent for Owner (Cat. No. 12).

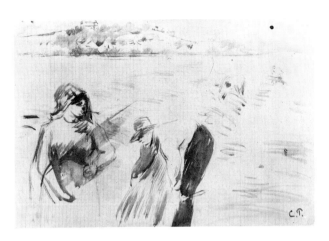

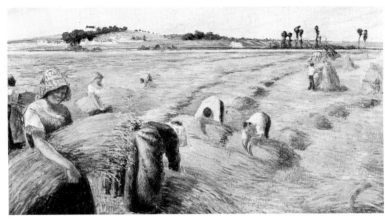

30 Camille Pissarro, *Study for The Harvest*, c.1882, brush and wash on squared paper, 27.5 × 47.8 cm. Ashmolean Museum, Oxford.

31 Camille Pissarro, *The Harvest*, 1882, tempera, 71 × 127 cm. National Museum of Western Art, Tokyo.

(Plate 55) has resolved drawings for both main figures to the lower left of *The Harvest*, drawn from life and developed from poses tested in the earlier versions of the ensemble. The final composition, with its high horizon, steep angle of vision, strong diagonals mapping empty space, figures both toiling and resting, repeated poses, and anchor figures to the lower left, reminds one of nothing so much as Degas's *Rehearsal* (Fig. 25). The fact that over a decade later Pissarro would recycle *The Harvest*'s main figure in a lithograph[66] is also reminiscent of Degas. However, Pissarro's cumbersome preparatory process and his landscape painter's preference for working from ensemble to accessory, rather than from drawn form to conceptual design, reveal his more empirical, less cerebral attitude to compositional drawing.

Degas's example was also important in encouraging a supple, simplified contour, which combined to give forms an independent strength without wrenching them from their surroundings as did the despotic outline of academic draughtsmen like Bouguereau. Since the late 1870s, monotonous handling and a timid bounding-line had led Pissarro almost to bury forms in the textured surface of his paintings. This could still be a problem as late as 1888, occurring, for all its fresh harmony of colour, in the gouache *Peasant Women in a Farmyard* (Fig. 32). Some time later, reworking these figures for an oil of the same motif,[67] Pissarro seems to have had in mind Degas's drawings for his sculpture *Little Dancer of Fourteen Years*, shown in 1881 (Fig. 33). Pissarro's drawing (Plate 72) explores the same model from two angles, and in fact the sheet is folded over at the right, where enough paper remains to draw another figure, as in Degas's tripartite studies. For all the difference of subject, the placement of the feet and vitality of the contour tell of the influence of Degas's drawing.

Gauguin's acceptance into the Impressionist circle in 1879 had been sponsored by Degas and Pissarro.

During the early 1880s he fell out with Degas over the internal politicking of the Impressionist exhibitions, Gauguin identifying with the landscape faction. By 1885 they had patched up their differences and Degas's draughtsmanship became for him, too, an important stimulus. In the summer of 1886 Gauguin made his first visit to Brittany, where the figure came to play an increasingly significant role in his landscapes, much as it had in the work of Pissarro. The most important canvas to result from this trip was the *Four Breton Women* (Fig. 34), which had its origins in a number of *croquis* made in a sketchbook and in two carefully worked drawings.[68] As the detail of modelling and costume suggests, these two sheets (Plate 10) were drawn from the model, probably local women dressed up in traditional costume for the benefit of touring artists. Gauguin's painting was indebted to Degas on several counts. Not only do the drawings share the sinuous yet firm quality of Degas's outlines, but two of Gauguin's poses seem to have been derived directly from Degas. The sheet in Glasgow appears to be indebted to a recollection of the *Study of a Dancer* (Fig. 35), then in the collection of Gauguin's friend Guillaumin, while the figure to the right of the painting owes something to another drawing by Degas in *essence* on pink paper which was shown at the second Impressionist exhibition, namely *Dancer Pulling on Her Slipper*.[69] The painting may not have been executed in Brittany but rather on Gauguin's return to Paris that autumn. Inventing a composition which incorporated individually realized poses in this fashion was of course one of Degas's procedures, as was the reusing of a pose, and the Breton peasant seen from behind, hands on hips, recurs several times in Gauguin's work over the next three years.

Another artist whose draughtsmanship had an impact almost equal to that of Degas was Puvis de Chavannes. Although Puvis cannot be considered an Impressionist, he was a longstanding friend of Morisot

30

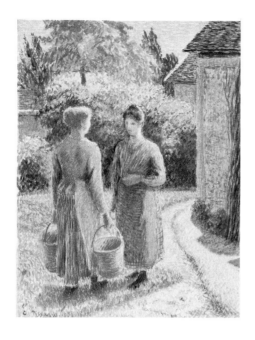

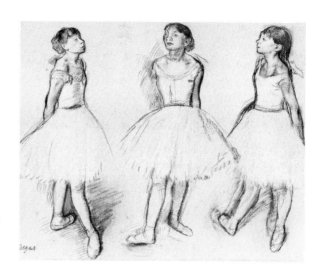

32 Camille Pissarro, *Peasant Women in a Farmyard*, 1888, gouache on silk, 32.5 × 24.6 cm. Metropolitan Museum of Art, New York.

33 Edgar Degas, *Study for Little Dancer of Fourteen Years*, c.1879–80, charcoal and pastel with stump, over graphite, heightened with white chalk, on buff paper, 48 × 61.6 cm. The Art Institute of Chicago, Chicago.

and Degas, and shared the Impressionists' chief dealer Durand-Ruel. He won honorary inclusion in Georges Lecomte's *L'Art Impressionniste* of 1892 (and in this exhibition) for the economy and the synthesis of his drawings.[70] During the 1880s Puvis was preoccupied with painting large mural canvases to decorate public buildings. His draughtsmanship and working practice were ordered to cope with such commissions, and his grand, calm compositions of arcadian subjects were much criticized by the academic establishment for precisely the qualities—sturdy linearity and lack of superfluous detail—that gained him the admiration of the avant-garde. Puvis's method was to think through an idea, while making rough sketches. Then, the idea fully formed in his mind, he rapidly encapsulated it in a large drawing of the ensemble, which would survive as the final composition with only minor adjustments. Finally, he worked on the constituent parts in more careful drawings, prior to the cartoon and the final painting.[71] To Puvis, creativity lay in the conception and in the drawing, not in the painting. The large drawing in Walsall (Plate 71) is the ensemble for *The Sacred Grove*, which was exhibited at the Salon of 1884 and was destined for the stairwell of the Musée des Beaux-Arts, Lyons. The drawing maps out the whole design, including, as in a later reduction (Fig. 36), the two flanks which at Lyons are on side walls, thereby settling in one energetic stroke both the composition and the value structure of the whole work. Puvis's easel paintings were also influential, and in the related drawings the synthetic force of his draughtsmanship is also apparent. In a pastel known as *Solitude* (Plate 73), linked in pose if not in iconography to a painting of *The Prodigal Son* (Fig. 37), Puvis too showed a willingness to reuse successful poses. In addition, the subdued tonality, active handling, cramped space and strong contours indicate how close he could come to an Impressionist contemporary like Pissarro (Plate 78).

Puvis was of considerable significance for young artists moving from academic training to independence during the 1880s. Seurat, for example, on leaving the École des Beaux-Arts developed a novel manner of drawing that was fully fledged by mid-1882 at the latest. By passing the rich, dark medium of conté crayon over the wispy surface of Michallet paper with the utmost manual dexterity, Seurat perfected a manner of supreme subtlety for conveying the effects of light.[72] This graphic style was quite contrary to academic procedures based predominantly on idealized outline, and was indebted to a variety of sources, not least the earlier tenebrist drawings of Millet (Fig. 12), Lebourg (Plate 60) and Lhermitte (Plate 38) and reproductions of Rembrandt etchings.[73] Seurat's first major figure-paintings—*Une Baignade, Asnières* (1883–4; London, National Gallery) and *La Grande-Jatte* (Fig. 38)—both recast Puvis's disciplined composition in a modern setting, and Seurat, who may well have had access to Puvis's studio, prepared his large canvases with similar attention. Unlike Puvis, Seurat preferred to work out his initial ideas not just in drawings but in painted sketches too. The drawing in the British Museum which fixed the landscape setting of *La Grande-Jatte* (Plate 58) also established the value structure of the whole design in black and white, as did Puvis's ensemble drawing for *The Sacred Grove*. Seurat's drawing emulated Puvis's advice to students about composition: 'Leave nothing to chance. Install your theatre, your stage, firmly, so it doesn't wobble . . . after that, it's embroidery.'[74] But when, in his haste to finish *La Grande-Jatte*, Seurat placed his figures on his 'stage', he did not employ a complete cartoon like Puvis. Another sheet in the British Museum (Plate 59) is in effect a 'cartoon' for the right-hand side only, combining figures and landscape elements previously explored in separate drawings. It is marked with indications in the margin to be squared into units that would correspond to half-metre sections of the main canvas, and these measurements match the inter-

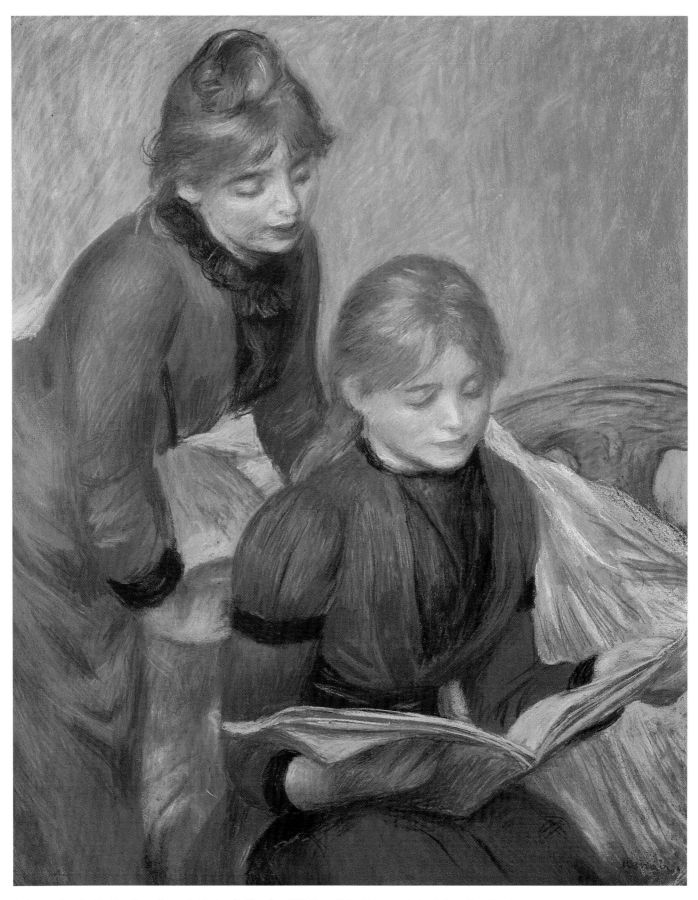

9 Auguste Renoir, *The Two Sisters* (formerly *The Lerolle Sisters*). *c*.1889. City of Bristol Museum & Art Gallery (Cat. No. 70).

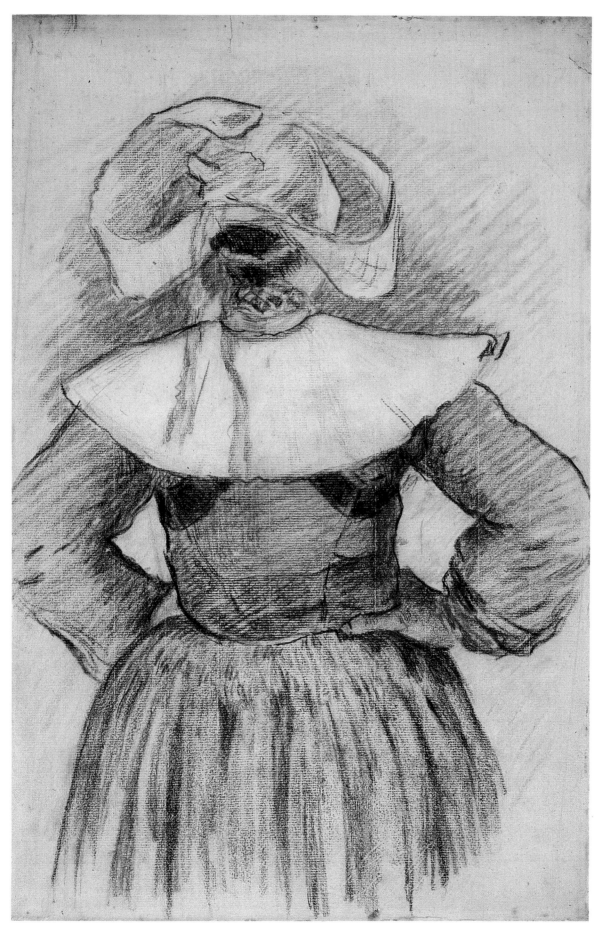

10 Paul Gauguin, *Study for Four Breton Women*. 1886. The Burrell Collection, Glasgow (Cat. No. 28).

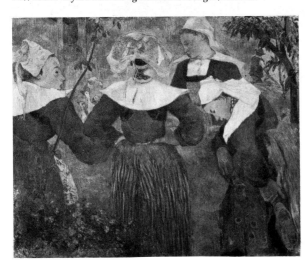

34   Paul Gauguin, *Four Breton Women*, 1886, oil on canvas, 71 × 90 cm. Bayerische Staatsgemäldesammlungen, Munich.

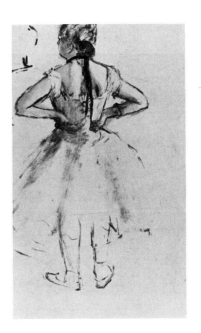

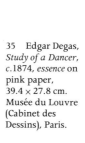

35   Edgar Degas, *Study of a Dancer*, c.1874, *essence* on pink paper, 39.4 × 27.8 cm. Musée du Louvre (Cabinet des Dessins), Paris.

mediary oil study for the right of the composition (Fig. 39). But Seurat did not take similar care with the left side of *La Grande-Jatte*, for which no 'cartoon' survives. On that side there are spatial and proportional discrepancies, and the harmony of the painting is marred by a failure that can be traced back to the neglect of drawing at a vital stage in the design.[75]

Although in the 1870s Renoir had at times used drawings as an aid to composition (Plate 54), his preference was still to use oil sketches. Even in the early 1880s, after a trip to Italy in 1881–2 to study Raphael and Pompeian frescos in an effort to strengthen his sense of form,[76] he continued to favour this approach. *Dance in the Country* (1882–3; Paris, Musée d'Orsay), for instance, seems to have been based on an oil sketch, and the drawings of the motif were probably made after the painting as studies for the reproduction in *La Vie Moderne*.[77] The disparate evidence about Renoir as a draughtsman points to a substantial increase in the number of drawings executed in the mid-1880s, many for compositional purposes. This is clear from the numerous studies for *Les Grandes Baigneuses* (1887; Philadelphia Museum of Art).[78] However, these figures were studied in isolation, both from each other—Renoir was not sufficiently confident to sustain the internal rhythms of groups—and from their environment, with the result that individual forms have a presence detrimental to the unity of the ensemble. Later, with the help of preparatory drawings, Renoir was able to resolve the problems of grouping figures. *The Promenade* of 1890 (Plate 77, Fig. 40) is indicative of this, with its simple, overlapping profiles reminiscent of *La Grande-Jatte*—an irony given Renoir's contempt for Seurat's painting. Drawing also came to serve Renoir as a convenient method for reworking earlier motifs. Studies like *The Snack* (Plate 37) of the early 1890s refined a composition initially attempted in the *Grape Pickers at Lunch* (Fig. 41) of 1884. The 1880s saw Renoir gradu-

ally reaping the benefits drawing could provide, even though his approach to composition was less conceptual than his colleagues'.

In terms of landscape painting, it is now well understood that the 1880s saw a growing withdrawal from the *plein air* work which had been so important to Impressionism in its early stages. Indeed, it seems likely that during the 1870s some canvases were retouched in the studio, and this trend grew with the concern for unity that so marked the new decade.[79] The emphasis on oil paint as the ultimate vehicle for the transcription of *sensation* in front of nature remained, with only Pissarro—as we shall see—prepared to dispute its primacy. Drawing thus tended to play the traditional subservient role in Monet's practice, for example. He seems to have used linear sketches (Fig. 19) simply to map out motifs and he occasionally returned to pastel, but he despised watercolour.[80] Sisley followed a similar pattern, though his notebooks are essentially *livres de raison* rather than preliminary observations,[81] and his production of landscape pastels (Plate 3), no doubt aimed at the market, seems on present evidence to have been greater. Cézanne, on the other hand, blossomed as a watercolourist in the 1880s. His practice of first establishing a motif with linear scaffolding and then building up discrete patches of colour whose warm-cool modulation gave form to the motif was one that paralleled and contributed to his experiments in painting, where the translucency of watercolour was replaced by packed planes of pigment.[82] Cézanne rigorously repeated motifs that fascinated him—the *sous-bois* (Plate 44) or *Mont Sainte-Victoire* (Plate 64)—over many years, amassing a repertoire of varied observations, and charting the chromatic changes of his chosen site.

The sequential exploration of landscape motifs had been a part of Impressionist practice prior to the 1880s, in painting as well as in drawing. Sisley's illustration of

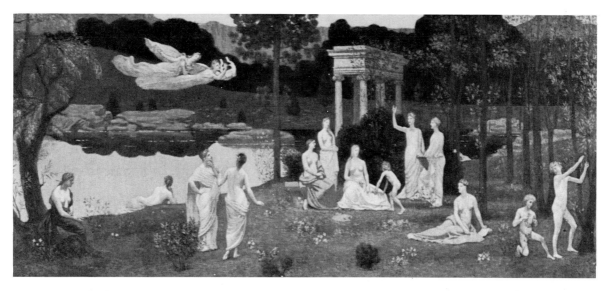

36 Pierre Puvis de Chavannes, *The Sacred Grove*, *c*.1884, oil on canvas, 92 × 210 cm. The Art Institute of Chicago, Chicago.

the *Point-du-jour* (Plate 80) repeated the motif of five canvases made in 1878, and in the mid-seventies Pissarro had made pastels of the same pond at Montfoucault in summer and autumn.[83] This practice flourished in the next decade. In 1888 Sisley showed a suite of six pastels at Durand-Ruel's, representing the railway station at Moret from slightly different angles and in different winter weather (Fig. 42). Restricted from working *en plein air*, he preferred pastel to oil for recording from indoors the rapidly changing meteorological conditions outside.[84] It was Pissarro who most actively applied graphic media to his landscape work during the 1880s, recommending watercolour to younger artists such as his son Lucien and to Signac,[85] and himself working frequently in tempera and pastel. He also deployed the greatest variety of media to the serial, seasonal observation of the same motif. One location on the downlands above his Eragny home can be first recorded on a fan of a harvest scene executed in gouache on silk and dated 1887;[86] the pastel *The Corn Stooks* (Plate 48) was probably a preliminary study. The following year Pissarro made watercolours of the same site after the field had been ploughed, and the annotation 'no. 14' on one of these sheets (Plate 46) suggests that it was part of a large group. The series culminated in a major oil, *The Gleaners* (Fig. 43), completed in 1889. In this case drawings served the conventional function of initial observation prior to more resolved work, but in acting as raw material for studio compositions they register a shift in Impressionist practice from the *plein air* doctrine to more studio-based work. Indeed, a composition such as *Female Peasant Planting Pea Sticks* (Plate 11) is more a dance-like vision of an agricultural arcadia than the close observation of a specific landscape.

As artists sought for greater unity and formal impact in their work so drawing was deployed more consciously. Its amplified importance is evident from different vantage points. There seems to have been an increasing use of sketchbooks—Pissarro used no less than thirteen in the eighties—and artists appear to have employed them deliberately at key moments in their careers—Renoir on his trips to Algeria and Italy in 1881–2, Gauguin in Brittany in 1886.[87] The substantial number of works on paper shown at the Impressionist exhibitions from 1879 bespeak a definite commitment to drawing; significantly the smallest number of drawings ever displayed was at the 1882 exhibition, which was dominated by landscape painters and lacked the Degas faction. The avant-garde's growing interest in the figure almost propelled drawing to the fore, and mentors such as Degas and Puvis ensured that its function was to serve the harmony of the ensemble. Above all, Impressionist artists saw drawing as inextricably linked to painting, a point emphasized by Gauguin in his *Notes Synthétiques* of *c*.1884.[88] Drawing led to synthetic form, which in turn contributed to a controlled, unified pictorial whole.

Drawing as Experiment

Perceptive reviewers of the Impressionist exhibitions recognized the degree of experimentation on show, and the role played by the graphic media. Degas had established himself as a pioneer, exhibiting drawings in *essence* on prepared pink paper in 1876 (Fig. 35), for instance, and pastels on monotype in 1877. His idea that work-in-progress or an essay in technique had an almost equivalent status to the finished painting became increasingly accepted in the Impressionist circle by the turn of the decade. Huysmans, for one, railed against the prejudice that disqualified Forain from serious consideration simply because watercolour, gouache and pastel were his preferred media, and he lauded the Impressionists for their innovations in mixed media and coloured frames.[89] Indeed, so complex and confusing did mixed media become that

35

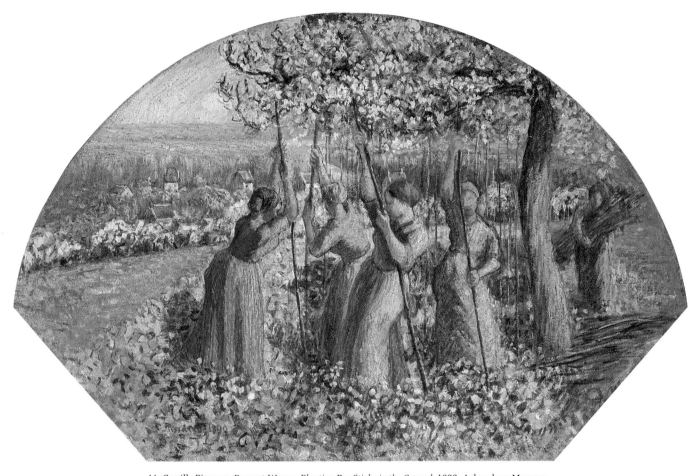

11 Camille Pissarro, *Peasant Women Planting Pea Sticks in the Ground*. 1890. Ashmolean Museum, Oxford (Cat. No. 59).

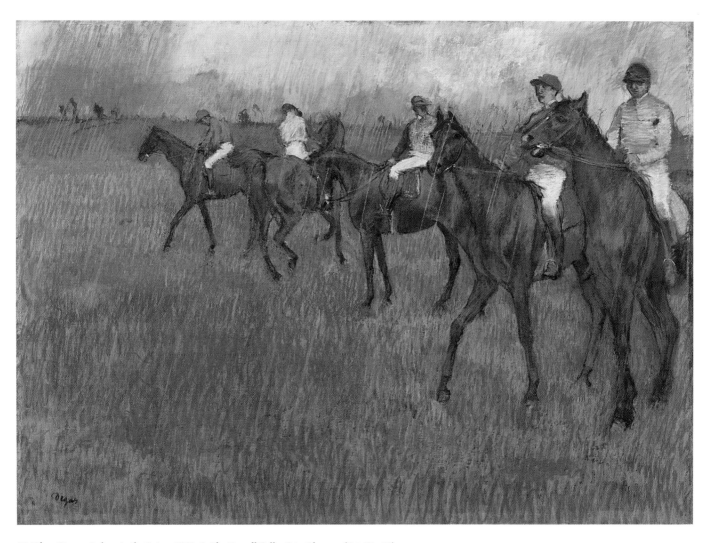

12 Edgar Degas, *Jockeys in the Rain*. *c*.1883–6. The Burrell Collection, Glasgow (Cat. No. 20).

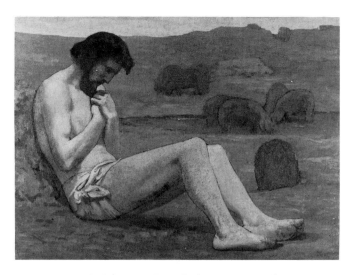

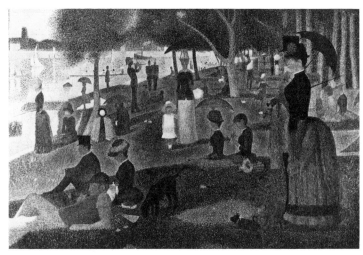

37   Pierre Puvis de Chavannes, *The Prodigal Son*, c.1879–82, oil on canvas, 106.5 × 146.7 cm. National Gallery of Art, Washington.

38   Georges Seurat, *Sunday on the Grande-Jatte (1884)*, 1884–6, oil on canvas, 225 × 340 cm. The Art Institute of Chicago, Chicago.

mistakes arose; in 1883 Pissarro complained bitterly when a critic mistook gouache for pastel.[90] However, the mixed application of graphic media was then practised in surprisingly wide artistic circles. The Aquarellistes, for instance, in the early 1880s, were divided about whether 'pure' watercolour mixed with the 'modern' medium of gouache was acceptable,[91] and Detaille was happy to exhibit drawings that mixed charcoal, pastel, gouache and other media in a manner worthy of Degas himself.[92]

The Impressionists' willingness to experiment was based not just on curiosity but practicality. One of the prime objectives in drawing is to make contours, which create a sense of space. The impermeable contour of pencil, the standard medium of academic practitioners like Gérôme and Bouguereau, allows no light. The reason, therefore, why Degas gradually abandoned pencil for black chalk as his chief graphic tool during the 1870s—to be followed by Pissarro around 1880—was because the more frangible contour created by chalk can actually hold light (Plates 34, 36). Seurat's adoption of conté in the early 1880s was for the same purpose, as was Renoir's use of sanguine (Plate 13), which had the additional recommendation of its suitability for the nude and its emulation of the rococo artists he so admired. Pissarro and Morisot at times made use of coloured crayons, especially in landscape drawings, to combine rapid delineation of the motif and colour notation.[93] This empirical attitude relates to other media too. Tempera, a hybrid between painting and watercolour, had been used in the 1870s by Degas, who had perhaps picked it up from theatrical circles, where it was widely used for scene painting.[94] Pissarro used tempera and gouache infrequently during the seventies, but on some 115 occasions in the 1880s;[95] they appealed to him—and indeed to a conservative such as the military painter de Neuville[96]—because their matt quality imitated pale natural light better than oil, and they required no

glossy varnish;[97] they also obviated the dense texture that Pissarro felt clogged his oil paintings.[98] These properties, and the possibility of distributing line and colour simultaneously with greater facility than oil, were shared with pastel, another medium whose popularity among the Impressionists greatly increased during the 1880s.

Innovation in the graphic and printmaking media had strong links in Impressionism. Duranty had recognized in 1876 that there was scarcely any distinction worth making between drawing and certain types of printmaking like drypoint.[99] In the seventies both the development of monotype and then the projected journal *Le Jour et La Nuit* had given tangible proof to Duranty's point.[100] Monotype is of greatest concern here, being a bastard medium, neither print nor drawing. Degas was not the only one to have experimented with it during the seventies—Lepic, for instance, had shown monotypes in 1876—but his use of this novel medium was the most challenging. Not only did he employ both the light field manner (drawing the image in ink on to the bare plate) and the dark field manner (wiping the ink from a fully covered plate to create the image) prior to printing, but he also allowed line and colour such a role that monotypes could combine the quintessence of graphic and of printed procedures. *Monsieur and Madame Cardinal* (Plate 53) may look a carelessly improvised print, but it involved line drawing before and after printing, its details of gesture having been first explored in sketches[101] and finally charcoal superimposed to sharpen the printed image. Degas, who may have known that Ingres had reworked and modified engravings after his pictures,[102] frequently retouched monotypes, etchings and lithographs with pastel to animate the monochrome motif.

Drawing could also overlap with experimental attitudes to painting. For instance, from the late 1870s first Monet and Degas, then Pissarro and Gauguin,

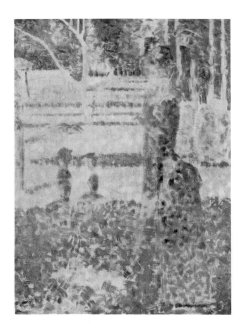

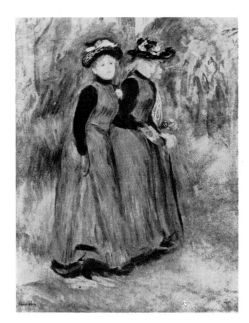

39 Georges Seurat, *Study for La Grande-Jatte: The Couple and Three Women*, c.1884–5, oil on canvas, 81 × 65 cm. Fitzwilliam Museum, Cambridge (on loan from the Keynes Collection, King's College, Cambridge).

40 Auguste Renoir, *The Promenade*, 1890, oil on canvas, 65 × 54 cm. Private Collection.

tried painting on square canvases, a notoriously tricky format,[103] which Pissarro also essayed in pastel (Plate 24). This treatment of drawing as a kind of laboratory inevitably gave it another status alongside that of direct observation of the natural motif that *croquis* and pastel had enjoyed in the previous decade. Thus by the mid-1880s Pissarro was using gouache as an indoor alternative to work *en plein air*. As he wrote to Lucien in July 1887: 'I do a session in the sun in the morning; the rest of the day I work on gouaches and my figure paintings.'[104] Work was divided into first- and second-hand activities, the latter done at one remove from reality via drawings or even Pissarro's own sculpture.[105] Furthermore, for all Cézanne's devotion to work *sur le motif*, his compositions of *Cardplayers* were founded as much on artificial sources—the watercolour of a head (Plate 7) taken from a cast in his studio—as from a posed model.[106] Drawing in the 1880s became the initial manifestation of the Impressionist painter's admission that his work was a conceptual interpretation rather than the instinctive reproduction of nature.

Drawing as Commerce

Inviting Degas to visit the Société d'Aquarellistes Vibert, a painter of detailed anecdotes of ecclesiastical gourmandise, admitted that if their gallery was luxurious it was because painting was 'un objet de luxe'. 'Yours may be,' retorted Degas, 'but ours are objects of prime necessity.'[107] Degas's remark was double-edged: he meant that Impressionist work was more sincere, and essential to the artists' livelihood. Underlying the commerce in drawings at this period lay two salient considerations. One was a shift in bourgeois taste. 'The art object replaces the work of art', complained one critic in 1880, and there was indeed a growing demand for the *bibelot*, the luxury item modest in scale to suit the middle-class apartment.[108] The other was the uncertain economic climate. After its spectacular recovery in the 1870s following the Franco-Prussian War, the French economy by the 1880s was weak again. The collapse of the Union Générale bank in 1882 hit Durand-Ruel badly,[109] and the Impressionists were forced to take the initiative in sales of their own work. In these circumstances, drawing had an important role. Collectors cautious about speculation in Impressionist painting might well risk works on paper; a drawing could be small yet valuable, attractive both as decor and as a low-risk investment.

The success of the Aquarellistes and later of the Société des Pastellistes Français, founded in 1885, was based on the market's demand for well-finished drawings. Items like Duez's *Hydrangeas* or Besnard's *Model* (Plates 62, 63), with their pleasing subjects and decorative designs, executed with great skill and a gesture to Impressionist procedures in their broad handling and *japoniste* off-centre compositions, scored great successes. Pastel was popular with collectors, and it was in artists' interests to use the medium. Indeed, Renoir's one-man-show at La Vie Moderne in 1879, and Manet's the following year, featured more pastels than oils, and at the 1886 Impressionist exhibition Pissarro showed a substantial group of peasant women and Degas a suite of women at their *toilette* (Plate 56; Figs. 46–50), all in pastel. In July 1886 Pissarro priced a number of works from that exhibition for Durand-Ruel, and listed pastels at 200 francs,[110] at a time when his own canvases were fetching two or three times that amount.[111] Degas's pastels went for much more. At the sale of the Dupuis collection in 1891 two nudes went for 2,100 francs and two more, including one from the 1886 exhibition, for 1,600 francs; nevertheless, an important painting by Degas could then fetch some 8,000 francs.[112] But pastels were quick to sell: Manet's *Two Women*

39

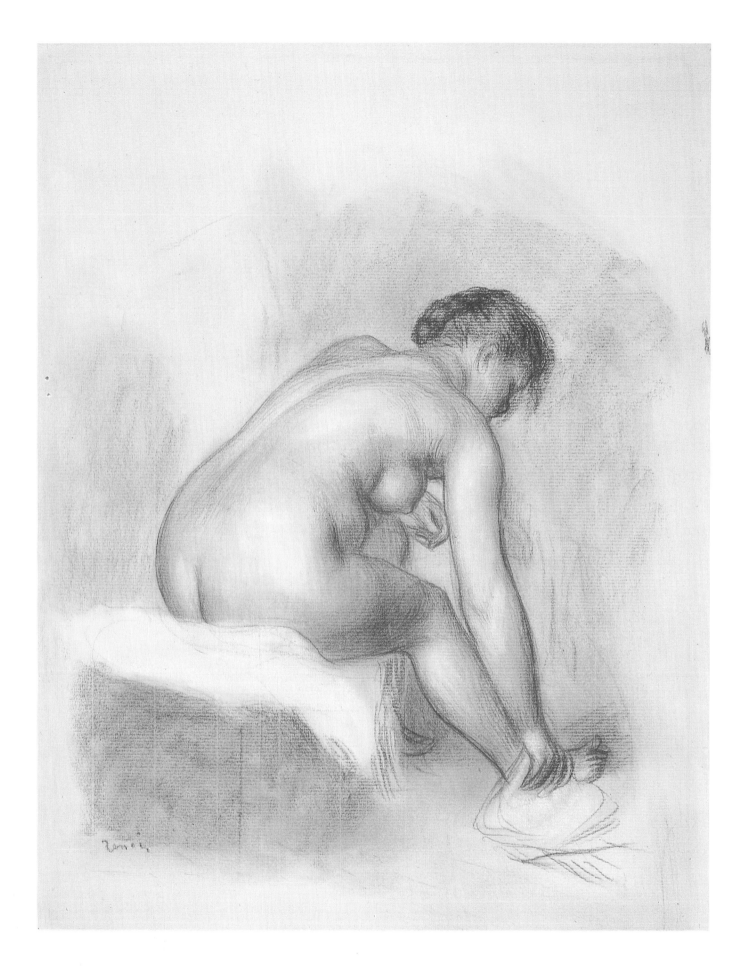

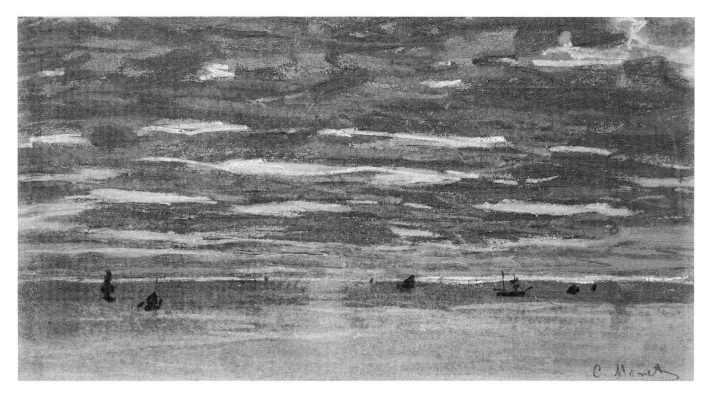

14 Claude Monet, *Sunset over the Sea*. 1865–70. Ashmolean Museum, Oxford (Cat. No. 42).

13 Auguste Renoir, *Nude Woman Seen from the Back*. 1885–90. British Museum, London (Cat. No. 68).

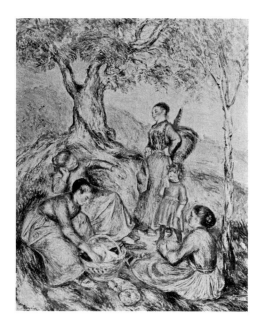

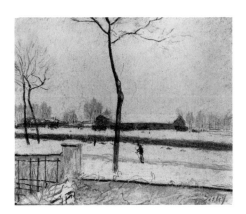

41 Auguste Renoir, *Grape Pickers at Lunch*, 1884, oil on canvas, 56 × 46 cm. Armand Hammer Foundation, Los Angeles.

42 Alfred Sisley, *The Railway Station at Moret: Snow*, 1888, pastel on brown paper, 45.8 × 54.7 cm. National Gallery of Scotland, Edinburgh.

Drinking Beer (Plate 17) sold from his exhibition to a Dutch collector; Degas's *Two Dancers in Their Dressing Room* (Fig. 28) was purchased by Edward Martyn in February 1886 at the instigation of George Moore;[113] and Manet's *Suzette Lemaire* (Plate 76) was commissioned following the success of an earlier pastel portrait of her for which he had been paid 1,000 francs.[114]

There was also a substantial market for watercolours and gouaches, and a highly finished watercolour by a recognized artist could reach a colossal sum. Puvis wryly recorded that while his huge decorative commission *The Sacred Grove* would earn him 40,000 francs, Detaille could get 30,000 for a single watercolour,[115] and Gustave Moreau was paid 1,000 or 1,500 francs for each of sixty-four watercolour illustrations to the *Fables* of La Fontaine that he did for the Marseilles collector Antoni Roux between 1881 and 1884.[116] Of the Impressionists it was Pissarro who most used watercolour as a breadwinner in the 1880s, and he certainly realized the difference between a study done for himself and 'une aquarelle *sérieuse*' made for the market.[117] Yet even late in the decade he was only able to get 500 francs for two topographical watercolours of Rouen.[118] Gouache, as a more obviously worked surface, had the commercial advantage of being a water-based medium with the appearance of oil; in 1885 Pissarro asked Durand-Ruel to sell *The Market Stall* (Plate 1) for 700 francs, the cost of a canvas.[119]

Painted fans, framed as decoration, enjoyed a considerable vogue in late nineteenth-century France. Manufacturers such as Desrochers, Alexandre and Duvelleroy mass-produced fans and commissioned designs from famous artists, while vast numbers were imported from Japan.[120] Fans proliferated at the Aquarellistes and Pastellistes. It was inevitable that the Impressionists should make them too, and at the 1879 exhibition Degas showed five, Forain four and Pissarro twelve. Both artists and dealers saw fans as supremely saleable. In 1882 Durand-Ruel wrote encouraging Pissarro to 'make small compositions in gouache on taffetta and fans',[121] and three years later Pissarro complained that he 'had got to churn out fans, because times are hard and for the moment one can only find a market for them, one mustn't count on paintings'.[122] Yet the prices they realized were modest. In the early 1880s Degas was taking 120 francs as top price, and even by 1890—perhaps even for fans as resolved as Plate 11—Pissarro was only able to ask 200 francs.[123]

From such evidence it seems apparent that the Impressionist artist was not able to rely on drawings alone for a living, but in times of hardship they could be used as a readily realizable commodity to supplement flagging income from painting. The artist had to recognize a hierarchy within the drawings market itself. This is clear from Pissarro's correspondence during the summer of 1884. In late June he asked Durand-Ruel to get 500 francs for two gouaches; by 12 August, still needing the same sum, he offered the minor dealer Heymann 'a series of watercolours and drawings heightened in coloured crayons'.[124] Clearly, different media had different market values, and it was to the artist's advantage to dispense appropriate work through dealers of contrasting cachet to the widest range of clientele.

Little is yet known about contemporary collectors of Impressionist drawings. From the haphazard evidence of owners of drawings in Impressionist exhibition catalogues, they appear to have been people from artistic, literary, journalistic and theatrical circles. Indeed, many might have lent drawings they had not bought but had been given, and Renoir for one was assiduous in using drawings during the eighties as gifts to influential writers like Théodore de Banville and Roger Marx as well as to dealers like Durand-Ruel and Portier.[125] Nevertheless, collectors of

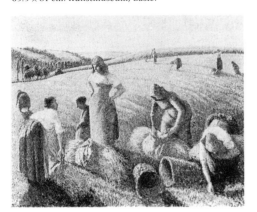

43 Camille Pissarro, *The Gleaners*, 1889, oil on canvas, 65.5 × 81 cm. Kunstmuseum, Basle.

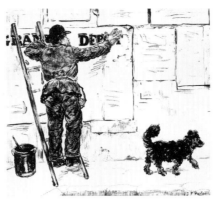

44 Jean-François Raffaëlli, *The Billsticker*, 1888, brush and ink, coloured crayons and watercolour, 50 × 57 cm. Sold Sotheby's, 2 July 1970 (3). Photo courtesy Sotheby's.

RIGHT 45 Edmé Bouchardon, *The Billsticker*, 1742, engraving. From: *Études prises dans le bas peuple, ou Les Cris de Paris*, Paris, 4th set, 1742.

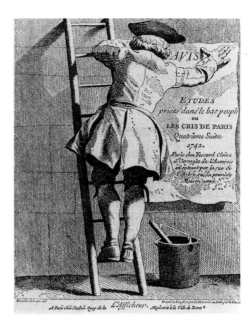

Impressionist paintings do seem to have recognized the status of drawing within the movement. Of the collection Gauguin built up between 1879 and 1881, twelve of the fifty items were drawings, some exchanged but others bought.[126] And Charles Ephrussi, wealthy owner of the *Gazette des Beaux-Arts*, had among his Impressionist canvases two fans by Pissarro, Manet's pastel portrait of Constantin Guys (New York, Metropolitan Museum) and at least one pastel by Morisot.[127]

The pastel portrait returned to popularity in the 1880s, achieving great commercial success. It was generally associated with the febrile refinements of the eighteenth century, and to some the revival of the genre's 'style télégraphique' was particularly suited to the rapid momentum of the modern age.[128] The opening exhibition of the Pastellistes in 1885 included works by Quentin de la Tour and Chardin to establish the ancestry of the modern pastel.[129] Manet's 1880 one-man-show featured many pastel portraits, to which he had turned partly for convenience given his failing health but also to rival successful practitioners of the genre like Chaplin.[130] Many of his sitters were women from the café society in which he moved— women such as Marie Colombier (Plate 40), a *demi-mondaine* who in the 1860s had been known as 'le plat du jour' and was soon to be literally horsewhipped by Sarah Bernhardt in retaliation for a malicious libel.[131] Manet's lively, luxuriant handling was emulated by followers like Gervex (Plate 61), who balanced pert treatment of the features against a briefly indicated background. Morisot and Degas were less concerned with working for the market. Morisot's portrait of the professional model Isabelle Lambert focuses on the face (Plate 67), while Degas's pastel catches the anxiety of his sitter's temperament by its acid combination of touches of lime-green and lavender on her face and by extending the format to include her tense body (Plate 4). Renoir's *Two Sisters*, typical of the Impressionists'

fusion of portraiture and the genre scene, is larger than his painting of this motif,[132] a reminder of the equivalent status drawing could have to painting (Plate 9).

Illustration too served a commercial end by publicizing artists' work to a broad public. As we have seen, new possibilities were opening up in the late 1870s, and the Impressionists were quick to exploit them. Degas and Cassatt had drawings reproduced in *Les Beaux-Arts Illustrés* in 1879, for example, and Somm in *Le Monde Parisien*.[133] Of notable importance was the establishment that year of the illustrated periodical *La Vie Moderne*, which was financed by the influential publisher Georges Charpentier. Degas, Cassatt, Manet, Forain, even Monet and Sisley were among the contributors. The journal did not pay its draughtsmen, and Renoir for one was content with the publicity it gave him at a time when he was keen to woo bourgeois patrons; in the summer of 1879 he even offered to produce weekly fashion illustrations. For him the chief drawback was working on Gillot paper, a medium which required the artist to scrape the image on a prepared surface.[134] Pissarro refused to contribute, since the use of the paper made it impossible to render purity of line.[135] Nevertheless, he attempted the technique, encouraging Lucien to try it, and had no deep-seated prejudice against illustration; in 1886 he tried to place two pen-and-ink drawings he had done in dots in illustrated magazines for 'quelques sous'.[136]

Abortive schemes for illustration abound in the history of Impressionism. In 1878 Manet's attempt to illustrate Cabaner's musical setting of Richepin's poems seems to have come to nothing, the scheme surviving in a handful of sketches (Plate 45). Two years later, despite a promotional article in *Le Gaulois* on its imminent appearance, *Le Jour et La Nuit* did not see the light of day;[137] neither did Degas's monotypes made at this time to illustrate Ludovic Halévy's *La Famille Cardinal*, and surely intended for publi-

43

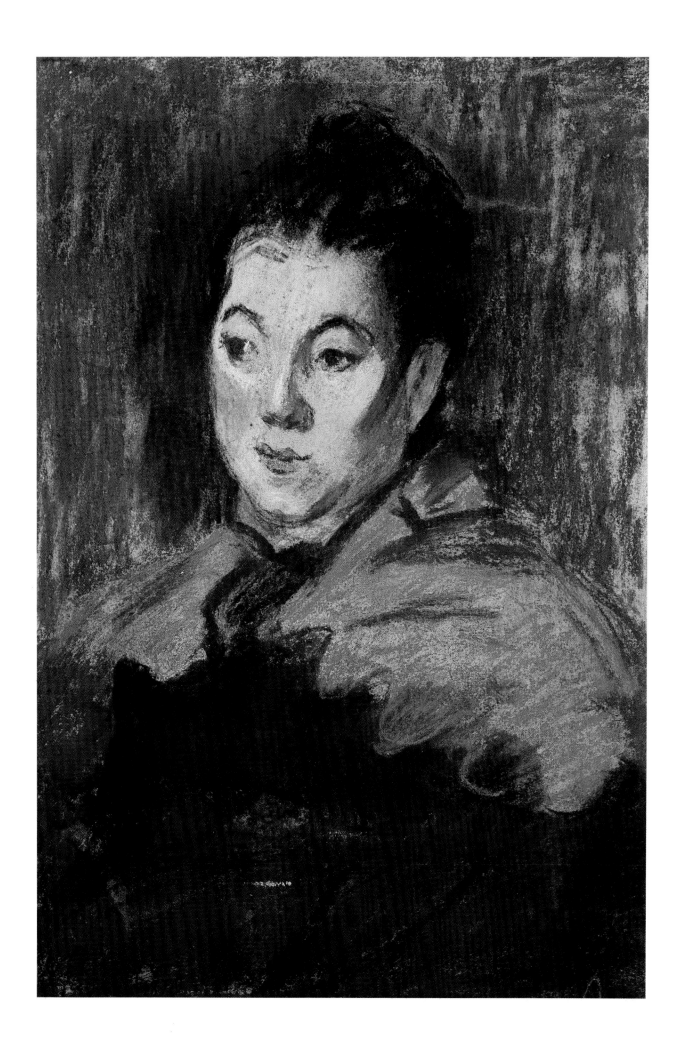

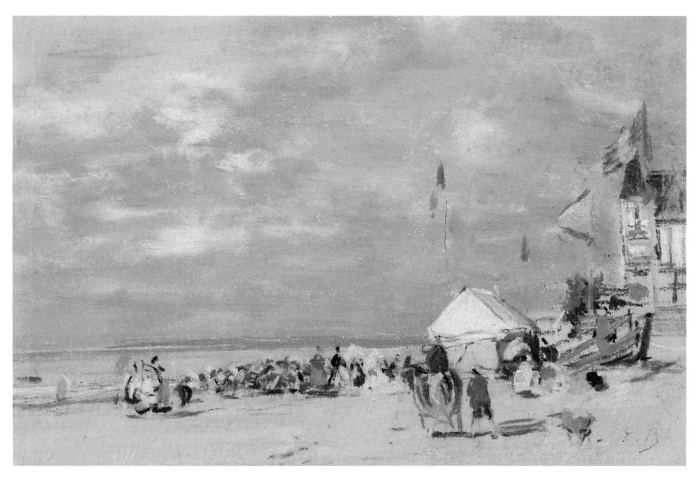

16 Eugène Boudin, *The Beach at Trouville with the Hôtel des Roches-Noires in the Background*. 1860–5. Private Collection (Cat. No. 3).

15 Camille Pissarro, *Portrait of Mlle Marie Daudon*. 1876. Ashmolean Museum, Oxford (Cat. No. 50).

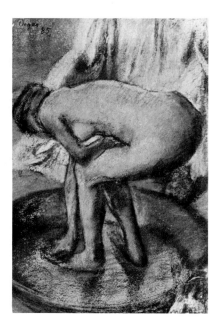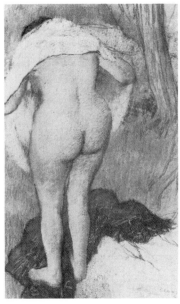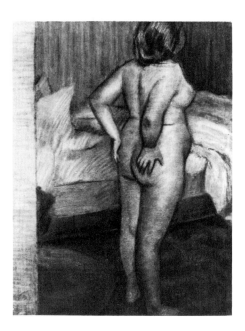

cation.[138] That there was an accepted role within Impressionism for illustration is indicated by Lucien Pissarro's submission at the 1886 exhibition, which included watercolours illustrating a traditional French song, *Il était une bergère* (Plates 49a–d), in the hope of attracting a publisher's interest, and a group of drawings for Octave Mirbeau's story *Les Infortunes de Maît'Liziard*, reproduced in *La Revue Illustrée* that June.[139] Commercial success as illustrators in general eluded the main Impressionists. It was however grabbed by Raffaëlli, a great self-publicist, with *Les Types de Paris*, a de luxe coloured album produced in 1889 with drawings accompanying short texts by writers like Maupassant, Huysmans and Richepin (Plate 51). Impressionist illustration succeeded best when the artist worked within standard systems; their experimental initiatives foundered. Nevertheless, illustration was more consistently practised than is usually realized.

Drawing and Meaning

Social observation has its place in Impressionist drawing, whether in sketches used to formulate the artist's first idea or in a highly finished sheet. The chief method of incorporating such meaning into figure subjects was by the standard device of the *type* or stock character, a tradition rooted in the graphic arts. This manner of documentary observation—depicting the figure with just sufficient detail of physiognomy, pose, role, and with perhaps the added evidence of a scantily indicated backdrop—had been current since the seventeenth century. Raffaëlli, for one, schooled himself in this tradition, and his *Billsticker* is a paraphrase of a figure from Bouchardon's *Études prises dans le bas peuple, ou les cris de Paris* (1742) (Figs. 44 and 45). The frequent appearance of the type in illustrated books and magazines made it a visual language for charting society and its changes easily

comprehended by wide audiences. Albert Wolff justified Raffaëlli's *Types de Paris* as classifying the 'entirely modern types' of the newly rebuilt city, and other critics responded to Impressionist subjects by reference to their types.[140] Types often occur as single figures, as in Somm's paradigmatic image (Plate 50) or Forain's amusing pastel of a hungover *boulevardier* (Plate 29). It was also an effective device in a crowd scene, acting as a register of social interchange. Forain excelled at this, above all in his sharply caricatural drawings of cafés and theatres with loitering whores and leering gentlemen (Plate 30).

Above all, the type was the key to wider meaning. When the caricaturist Bertall raged against 'such frightful and vulgar types . . . this series of women drinking beer'[141] at Manet's one-man-show he recognized that Manet's women, like Somm's *Beer Waitress* (Plates 43, 50), evoked a complex of economic, even moral, issues within the social order of Paris. At this period cafés and brasseries were increasingly used as illicit cover for unregistered prostitutes.[142] With the suggestive gesture linked to payment and the tricolour costume implying that the *femme de brasserie* typified the working-class Parisienne, Somm made play with this knowledge. So did Manet, with his apparently preoccupied women waiting to be picked up (Plate 17). The cripple which he included in a street-scene hung with flags celebrating the 1878 Universal Exhibition and France's recovery after the Franco-Prussian War acted as an emblem of the cost of that conflict—an irony reinforced by the caption on a *croquis* (Plate 45).[143] Similarly, in his drawings for *La Grande-Jatte* Seurat froze his types into a rigidity of attitude that would be central to the painting's meaning (Plate 59).[144]

Landscape drawing could also be invested with meaning. Sisley's *Point-du-jour* (Plate 80) was based on a painting which, with its concentration on the Trocadéro, fluttering tricolours, and crowds outside

46

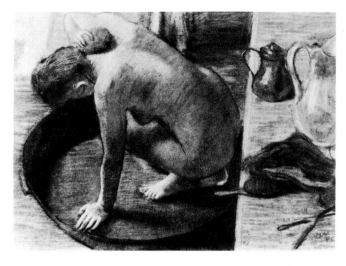

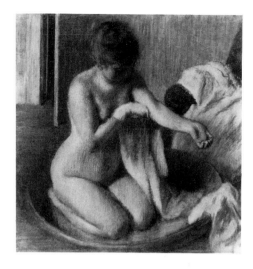

49 Edgar Degas, *The Tub*, 1886, pastel, 60 × 83 cm. Musée d'Orsay, Paris.

50 Edgar Degas, *Woman in a Tub*, c.1885–6, pastel, 68 × 68 cm. Tate Gallery, London.

the Grand Concert Cadran, proclaimed the success of the 1878 Universal Exhibition.[145] Again, the initial drawings of the motif of Pissarro's *Harvest* (Fig. 30) testify to his consistent intention to include on the distant hill the château which dominates the village and the peasants who work their landlord's open fields.

Coda: Degas in 1886

The newly claimed importance of draughtsmanship, the refined synthesis of form, and the deployment of contemporary meanings were powerfully distilled in the single most important group of drawings shown at the Impressionist exhibitions: the 'Suite of nudes of women bathing, washing, drying or wiping themselves, combing their hair or having it combed' submitted by Degas in 1886. Ten pastels were so listed in the catalogue, and there has been confusion about which and how many were actually shown. Gustave Geffroy's authoritative review, published eleven days after the opening of the exhibition, described only six, which can now be identified: the images were of the woman 'bending over, straightening out in her tub, feet reddened by the water (Fig. 46), sponging her neck, raised on her short massive legs (Fig. 49), stretching out her arms to put on her chemise (Fig. 47), drying herself, on her knees, with a towel (Fig. 50), standing up, head squat and rump stuck out (Fig. 48), or tipped over to one side (Plate 56)'.[146] These identifications are corroborated by other critics, above all Fénéon, who in his slightly later review described a seventh pastel which showed three women and a dog bathing in a river.[147] This image, which seems to have been lost, must have been added midway through the exhibition. It thus appears that only seven of the planned pastels were actually shown.

The critical response was positive. Above all, the quality of draughtsmanship was praised unanimously, with Mirbeau stressing the 'synthetic power, the linear abstraction'.[148] It was Geffroy, followed by Fénéon, who was the first to make the now clichéd point that Degas depicted 'the woman *who does not know she is being looked at*, as one would see her hidden behind a curtain or through a keyhole'.[149] Significantly, critics were ambiguous about who these women were. One figure was picked out as bourgeoise (Fig. 48),[150] and writers veered from stating that they were prostitutes to using unspecific terms like 'slut'.[151] Several adopted the allusive term 'batracienne', meaning 'amphibian' or, loosely, 'frog'.[152] This was a double-edged reference: in one sense it referred to the way the women were posed in certain pastels, for instance in the Burrell *Tub* (Plate 56), where the hunched back pulled down over the thighs bore a physical resemblance to a creature such as a frog. But in the 1880s 'frog' was used in slang references to mercenary sex; prostitutes working in Latin Quarter cafés were known as 'les grenouilles de brasserie'.[153] A contemporary vignette by Galice (Fig. 51) represented a buxom woman *en déshabillé* catching a frog on a line, fishing being a common metaphor for prostitution.[154] Critics were aware of Degas's using 'current metaphors' in these pastels, and his implicit analogies between the curvaceous bodies of bathing women and the upholstered furniture (Fig. 50) or rounded jugs (Figs. 46 and 49) with which they are often juxtaposed stimulated stock masculine associations about the female body as a passive sexual object.[155] Degas's suite of nudes was thus a fertile combination of virtuoso technique and subtle allusion to popular meanings.

Conclusion

By the mid-1880s Impressionist artists shared an increasing tendency to produce related groups of work, linked by motif or medium. The 1886 exhibition included suites of pastels by Degas, Pissarro and

47

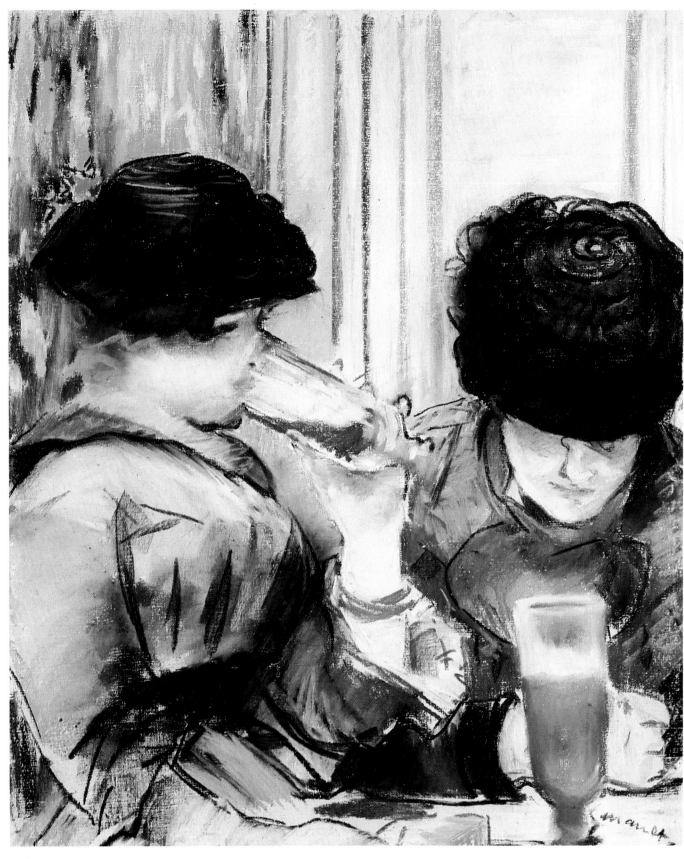

17 Édouard Manet, *Two Women Drinking Beer (Les Bockeuses)*. 1878. The Burrell Collection, Glasgow (Cat. No. 39).

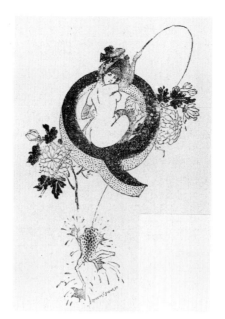

51 Galice, Vignette from A. Silvestre,
Le Nu au salon de 1889, Paris, 1889, n.p.,
1889, wood engraving, 9.5 × 6 cm.
Private Collection.

Zandomenghi and series of drawings and watercolours by Morisot; that year, too, Morisot admired a group of drawings after the same model in Renoir's studio.[156] For many Impressionists drawing had become a more effective means of exploring a sequential idea or of synthesizing an individual form than painting. During the 1880s artists were no longer so concerned to record a variety of naturalistic observations, but strove instead to arrive at quintessential forms in a fashion that was much admired by the young Symbolist generation. Drawing, with its inherent linearity, fluency and economy, was perhaps the key vehicle in this development; it stood at a complex conjunction of concerns. Pissarro's *Market Stall* (Plate 1) is an apposite example since it can be read on several levels. It needs to be understood in terms of technique, as a figure subject employing Degas's spatial daring and sinuous contour while not abandoning Pissarro's own *naïveté*, and as the application of media that would circumvent Pissarro's problems with oil; in commercial terms, as a highly resolved sheet with the status and price of a painting; and in socio-economic terms, with the sturdy butcher girl set against the sick *bourgeoise* in a juxtaposition of class and an image of transaction typical of Pissarro's market scenes.[157] In the context of Impressionism, drawing ceased to be a peripheral activity limited to preparatory work or immediate observation. It became a vital element in Impressionist practice, a means of achieving synthesis of form, a vehicle for fertile experimentation with media, a source of financial gain, and a sophisticated instrument of social observation.

RICHARD THOMSON

Notes

1. Pevsner, 1940, remains the standard account, but for the later century see now Boime, 1971, especially Chapter 1. The quotation from Lebrun can be found in Fontaine, [1903], p. 39.
2. Ingres, 1863, p. 8.
3. Boime, 1971, p. 21.
4. Boime, 1977, pp. 1–39.
5. Boime, 1969, p. 414.
6. For the unreformed École des Beaux-Arts see Grunchec, 1983, and for the reforms Boime, 1977, pp. 11–18.
7. Two reproductions (a photograph and a lithograph) of the drawing by Signorelli are recorded in Cézanne's studio (Reff, 1960, p. 304).
8. Lichtenstein, 1964, pp. 55–67, 425–6 and Lichtenstein, 1975, pp. 116–27.
9. Ballas, 1974, pp. 193–7 and Ballas, 1981, pp. 223–31.
10. Nathansan and Olszewski, 1980, pp. 243–55.
11. Delaborde, 1870, and Amaury-Duval, 1878.
12. Boime, 1980, especially pp. 458–72.
13. *Charles Gleyre*, 1974–5, particularly the essay by Boime, pp. 102–24, and *Charles Gleyre*, 1980.
14. Boime, 1976, pp. 189–90 and Fehrer, 1984, pp. 207–16.
15. Mack, 1935, pp. 104–5 quoting Dubuisson, *Paris-Midi*, 2 January 1925.
16. Summaries of the controversy can be found in Boime, 1971, pp. 181–4, and Boime, 1977, pp. 19–23. For a new edition of the texts by Vitet and Viollet-le-Duc see Foucart, 1984.
17. Viollet-le-Duc, 1864 (Foucart, 1984, p. 95) echoing a passage in Horace Lecoq de Boisbaudran, 1911, p. 86, for whom see below.
18. Ibid.
19. Viollet-le-Duc, 1862, p. 526 (Foucart, 1984, p. 116).
20. Viollet-le-Duc, 1864 (Foucart, 1984, p. 97).
21. ten-Doesschate Chu, 1982, pp. 242–89.
22. The English edition of Lecoq de Boisbaudran's main published works issued with the title *The Training of the Memory in Art* (1911) is still the most useful and accessible.
23. For example, the copy by Lhermitte in the Victoria and Albert Museum (acc. no. 5942) after an altarpiece by Titian (H. Wethey, *The Paintings of Titian, The Religious Paintings*, London, 1969, vol. 1, Cat. no. 56).
24. The impact of Lecoq de Boisbaudran's theories is discussed by ten-Doesschate Chu, 1982, pp. 281–7. For the influence on Manet see Wechsler, 1978, pp. 32–4; for Degas see Reff, 1976, vol. 1, p. 141, Nb. 34, p. 7; for Pissarro see *Pissarro Correspondance*, 1980, p. 35.
25. Lecoq de Boisbaudran, 1911, pp. 77 and 85.
26. Tucker, 1985, pp. 465–76.
27. The main reviews are reprinted in *Centenaire de l'impressionnisme*, 1974, pp. 256–70. Émile Cardon writing in *La Presse* is an example of an uncomprehending reviewer, while Philippe Burty in *La République française* was more searching.
28. *Centenaire de l'impressionnisme*, 1974, pp. 268–70.
29. *Centenaire de l'impressionnisme*, 1974, pp. 264–5.
30. See the essay by Isaacson in *Crisis of Impressionism*, 1979–80, pp. 2–47. A contemporary reviewer such as Charles Bigot writing in *La Revue politique et littéraire* (p. 1046) of 1877 was alive to these divisive factors.
31. For a useful list of the participants in the eight exhibitions see Rewald, 1973, p. 591.
32. Isaacson in *Crisis of Impressionism*, 1979–80, pp. 4–6.
33. Duranty, 1876, pp. 24–5.
34. For a survey of Realist and Naturalist drawing see the essay by ten-Doesschate Chu in *The Realist Tradition*, 1980, pp. 21–38.
35. A statistical breakdown of the drawings included in the eight Impressionist exhibitions provides the following result:

	number of works exhibited	drawings*
1874	165	38
1876	248	29
1877	241	30
1879	246	80
1880	232	60
1881	170	50
1882	203	28
1886	246	71

*clearly marked as 'aquarelle', 'pastel', 'éventail': items framed together or under one number counted once

36. On pastels see Monnier, 1984.
37. For a survey of the watercolour landscape tradition in nineteenth-century France see the essay by de Leiris in *From Delacroix to Cézanne*, 1977–8, pp. 16–68.
38. On Cézanne's watercolours see Rewald, 1983.
39. Baudelaire, 1965, pp. 199–200.
40. For the works by Goeneutte see Alley, 1981, pp. 289–90 and for Buhot see *Félix Buhot*, 1983–4, nos. 57a and 85a. Compare also Van Gogh's renditions of the same boulevard recorded in two drawings (J. Hulsker, *The Complete Van Gogh*, Oxford, 1980, nos. 1217 and 1219).
41. Reff, 1976.
42. For Monet's sketchbooks see Isaacson, 1978, p. 206, no. 43ff. and for Sisley's see Wildenstein, 1959, pp. 57–60.
43. Rewald, 1946.
44. Venturi, 1939, II, p. 337.
45. Lemoisne, 399.
46. Lemoisne, 537 and also Frick Collection, II, 1968, pp. 82–6.
47. See the essay by Shackelford in Washington, 1984, pp. 85–107.
48. See *Degas, 1879*.
49. Havard, 1879, p. 3.
50. Huysmans, 'Le Salon de 1879', *Oeuvres complètes, VI*, 1929, pp. 10–11, n. 1.
51. Havard, 1879, p. 3.

52. Lostalot, 1879, pp. 82–3; Reff, 1976, I, p. 136 (Nb. 31, pp. 93, 92).
53. See n. 35 above.
54. *Pissarro Correspondance*, 1980, p. 96, n. 3 (letter of 14.12.1874).
55. Bodelsen, 1968, p. 339.
56. Baignères, 1879, pp. 491–2; *Soc. d'Aquarellistes Français*, 1883, I, p. 91.
57. Martelli, 'Correspondances', *Roma Artistica*, 15 April 1879 (Martelli, 1979, pp. 107–8).
58. Chardin, 1879, p. 421.
59. Lostalot, 1882, p. 176.
60. Michel, 1884. No Impressionists were included.
61. Fourcaud, 1884, p. 106.
62. Adam, 1886.
63. Reff, 1976, I, p. 134 (Nb. 30, p. 210).
64. *Degas, 1879*, pp. 9–15.
65. B/L 122; P & V 1558.
66. Delteil, 1923, no. 141.
67. P & V 1272.
68. See cat. 28 below.
69. Private collection; repr. *Degas. Pastelle, Ölskizzen, Zeichnungen*, 1984, no. 97.
70. Lecomte, 1892, pp. 179–89.
71. Vachon, 1900, pp. 84–91.
72. Herbert, 1962, pp. 35–57; Thomson, 1985, pp. 23–32.
73. Broude, 1976.
74. Vachon, 1900, p. 99.
75. Thomson, 1985, pp. 97–114.
76. White, 1969.
77. For the oil sketch see Daulte, 1971, no. 439, and for the drawings Rewald, 1946, nos. 13, 15, 16, 18.
78. White, 1973.
79. See *inter alia* J. House, 'The Legacy of Impressionism in France', in *Post-Impressionism*, 1979–80, pp. 13–18.
80. For *croquis*, see for example Isaacson, 1978, nos. 77, 79, 80; pastel, *The Cliff at Etretat* (Paris, Musée Marmottan, inv. 5034); and for watercolour, Puget, 1957, p. 79.
81. Wildenstein, 1959.
82. Elderfield, 1971; *Watercolour and Pencil Drawings by Cézanne*, 1973.
83. Daulte, 1959, nos. 85, 295–8; P & V 1525, 1527.
84. For this group see Venturi, II, 1939, p. 62 (letter of 17 May 1888) and F. Fénéon, 'Quelques Impressionnistes', *La Cravache*, 2 June 1888 (Fénéon, 1970, p. 127).
85. For instance Pissarro, 1950, p. 246 (letter of 13 May 1891) and Besson, 1950, p. 8 (letter of 30 August 1888).
86. P & V 1639.
87. B/L XI–XXIII; *Renoir: Carnet de dessins*, 1955; *Paul Gauguin: Carnet de croquis*, 1962.
88. *Paul Gauguin: The Writings of a Savage*, 1978, pp. 11–12.
89. Huysmans, 'L'Exposition des Indépendants en 1881', *Oeuvres complètes*, VI, 1929, pp. 272–5.
90. *Pissarro Correspondance*, 1980, pp. 206–7 (letter of 13 May 1883).
91. Privat, 1881, p. 356; Baignères, 1882, p. 434.
92. *Soc. d'Aquarellistes Français*, 1883, I, p. 70.
93. E.g. Pissarro, *Landscape at Pontoise* (Paris, Louvre, Cabinet des Dessins, RF 28801); Morisot, *Spring Landscape* (Washington, National Gallery of Art, inv. 25485).
94. Moynet, 1874, p. 118.
95. P & V 1329–1442, 1444.
96. *Soc. d'Aquarellistes Français*, I, pp. 6, 203.
97. Callen, 1982, pp. 62–3.
98. *Pissarro Correspondance*, 1980, p. 202 (letter of 4 May 1883).
99. Duranty, 1876, p. 30.
100. *Degas Monotypes*, 1968; *Degas: The Painter as Printmaker*, 1984–5, pp. xxxix–lv.
101. Reff, 1976, I, pp. 126–7 (Nb. 27, pp. 3, 4, 6).
102. *In Pursuit of Perfection*, 1983–4, p. 27.
103. Callen, 1982, p. 60.
104. Pissarro, 1950, p. 157 (letter of 6 July 1887).
105. Thomson, 1983.
106. Reff, 1980; Rewald, 1984, no. 378.
107. Vollard, 1924, pp. 26–7.
108. Claretie, 1881, pp. 25–7 (entry of 22 March 1880); Saisselin, 1985.

109. Boime, 1976, p. 169.
110. Venturi, 1939, II, p. 22 (letter of 7 July 1886). At this period an average artisan's wage was 100–150 francs per month; an exceptional year on the Stock Market brought Gauguin 35,000 francs.
111. Rewald, *Gazette des Beaux-Arts*, 1973, pp. 102–3.
112. Ibid., pp. 76, 89–90. *La Femme au tub* (Fig. 50) was either no. 12 or 15 in the Dupuis sale.
113. *Drawings from the National Gallery of Ireland*, 1967, no. 89.
114. Tabarant, 1947, p. 429.
115. *Puvis de Chavannes*, 1977, p. 194 (letter of 20 August 1883).
116. Mathieu, 1977, p. 274, n. 535.
117. *Pissarro Correspondance*, 1980, p. 141 (letter of 23 December 1880).
118. *Archives*, 1975, no. 189 (letter from Theo Van Gogh, 16 February 1889).
119. *Pissarro Correspondance*, 1980, p. 335 (letter of early June 1885).
120. Uzanne, 1882, p. 126; Boime, 1976, p. 180; Gerstein, 1982, p. 107.
121. Venturi, 1939, I, p. 62 (letter of December 1882).
122. *Pissarro Correspondance*, 1980, p. 359 (letter of 12 December 1885).
123. Gerstein, 1982, p. 109; Venturi, 1939, II, p. 40 (letter of 30 November 1890).
124. *Pissarro Correspondance*, 1980, pp. 307, 312 (letters of late June and 12 August 1884).
125. Daulte, 1958, nos. 3, 6, 9, 16.
126. Bodelsen, 1970, nos. 3, 10–14, 20, 22, 27, 31, 35, 43.
127. *Oeuvres Complètes de Jules Laforgue*, 1925, p. 88 (letter of 9 January 1882). The Morisot was *Dans le parc*, Paris, Petit Palais, inv. P.P.P.746.
128. Vielcastel, 1881; Gilbert, 1886.
129. Mirbeau, 'Les Pastelistes Français', *La France*, 9 April 1885 (Mirbeau, 1922, pp. 33–4).
130. Blanche, 1919, p. 137.
131. Goncourt, 1956, VII, p. 54 (26 February 1865); Sutton, 1961, pp. 66–7.
132. Daulte, 1971, no. 562.
133. See *Les Beaux-Arts Illustrés*, 10, 1879, p. 84; *Le Monde Parisien*, 14, 29 March 1879, p. 1.
134. Rewald, 1945, pp. 183–8. For gillotage see also *Degas: The Painter as Printmaker*, 1984–5, pp. xxxiii–v, xliii–xlvi, figs. 9, 21–2, 27, 29.
135. *Pissarro Correspondance*, 1980, p. 282 (letter of 10 February 1884).
136. Lloyd, 1980; Pissarro, 1950, p. 117 (letter of 27 December 1886).
137. *Degas: The Painter as Printmaker*, 1984–5, pp. xxxix–lv.
138. *Degas Monotypes*, 1968, pp. xxi–xxiii; Adhémar/Cachin, 1974, pp. 87–8.
139. *La Revue Illustrée*, 15 June 1886, pp. 457–64.
140. Wolff, 1889, pp. I–II; d'Hervilly, 1879; Ephrussi, 1880, p. 486; anon., 1886.
141. Bertall, *L'Artiste*, 1 May 1880 (Hamilton, 1954, p. 229).
142. Gronberg, 1984.
143. Rouart/Wildenstein, I, no. 270; Collins, 1975.
144. Thomson, 1985, pp. 115, 121–3.
145. Thomson, 1981[2].
146. Geffroy, 1886.
147. F. Fénéon, 'VIIIe Exposition Impressionniste', *La Vogue*, 13–20 June 1886 (Fénéon, 1970, p. 30).
148. Mirbeau, 1886, p. 1.
149. Geffroy, 1886; Fénéon, 1970, p. 31.
150. Ajalbert, 1886, p. 386; Huysmans, *Oeuvres complètes*, X, p. 22.
151. Fevre, 1886, p. 154; anon., 1886.
152. Fénéon, 1970, p. 30; Adam, 1886, p. 545.
153. Carel, 1884, p. 2.
154. Thomson, 1985, pp. 123–4.
155. R. Thomson, 'Notes on Degas's Sense of Humour' (Kendall, 1985, pp. 14–15). See also A. Gruetzner, 'Degas and George Moore' (ibid., pp. 33–6).
156. *Correspondance de Berthe Morisot*, 1950, p. 128 (11 January 1886).
157. Lloyd, 1985, pp. 24–5.

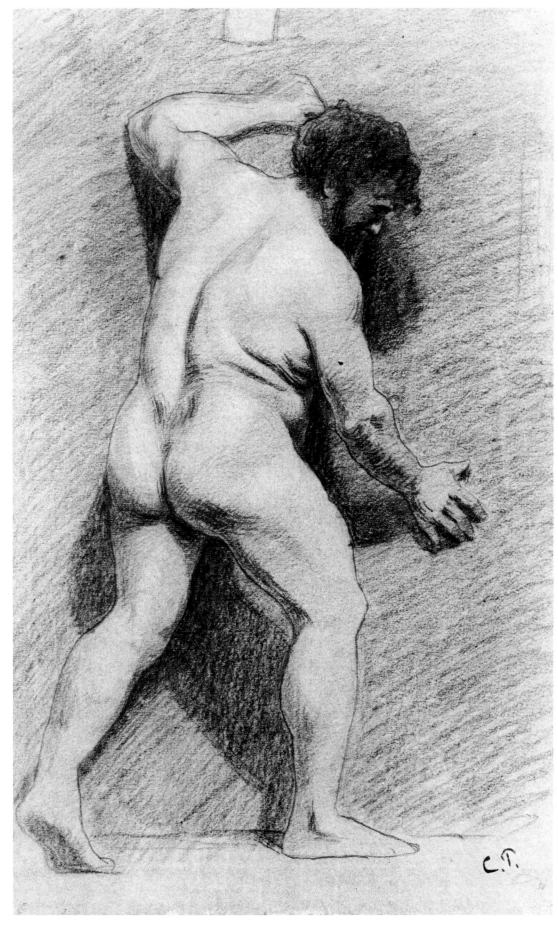

52

18 Camille Pissarro, *Study of a Male Nude Posed against a Wall Seen in Profile Facing Right*. 1855–60. Ashmolean Museum, Oxford (Cat. No. 46).

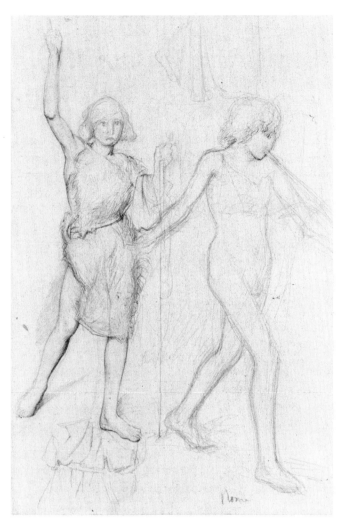 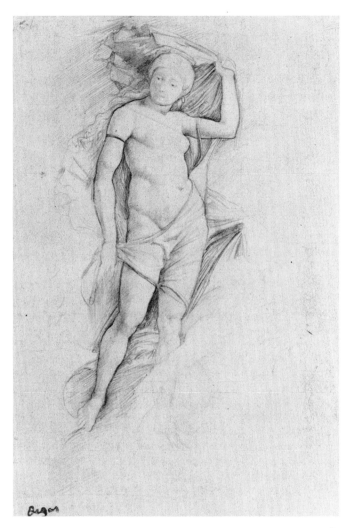

19 Edgar Degas, *Studies for 'St John the Baptist and the Angel'*. 1856–8. Ashmolean Museum, Oxford (Cat. No. 14).

20 Edgar Degas, *Venus* (after a figure from the painting *Pallas Expelling the Vices* by Andrea Mantegna). *c*.1855. Ashmolean Museum, Oxford (Cat. No. 13).

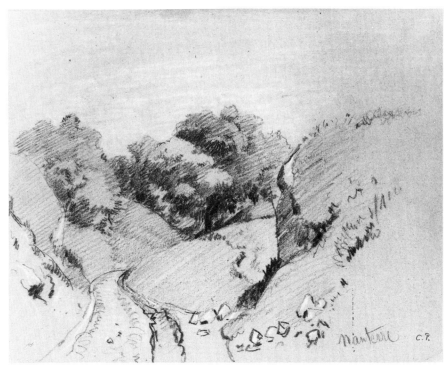

21 Camille Pissarro, *Nanterre. c.*1860. Ashmolean Museum, Oxford (Cat. No. 48).

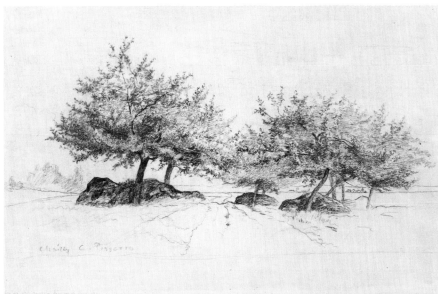

22 Camille Pissarro, *Chailly. c.*1857. Ashmolean Museum, Oxford (Cat. No. 47).

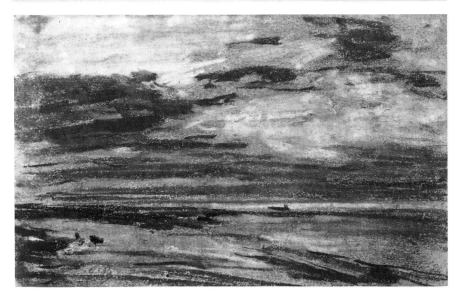

23 Louis-Eugène Boudin, *Sunset over the Sea*. 1860–70. Fitzwilliam Museum, Cambridge (Cat. No. 2).

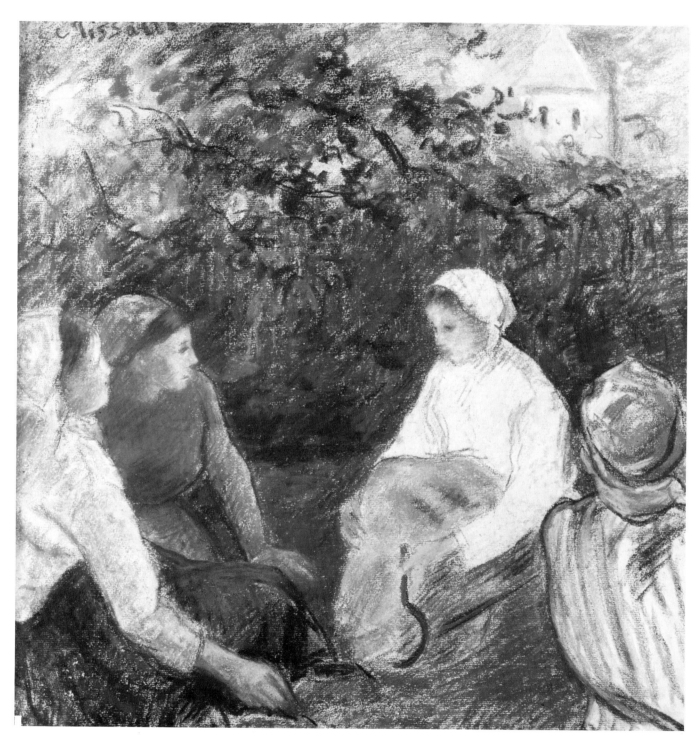

24 Camille Pissarro, *Four Seated Peasant Women*. c.1885. Private Collection (Cat. No. 56).

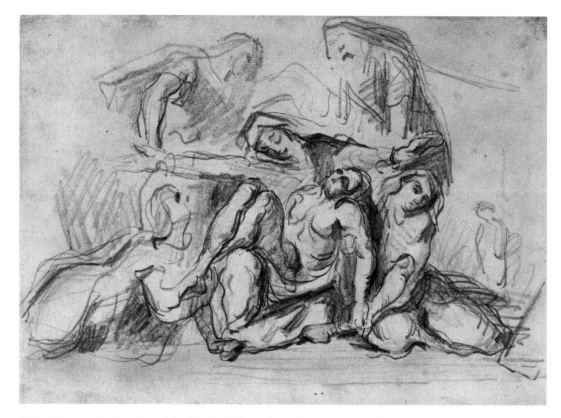

25 Paul Cézanne, *The Entombment* (after the painting by Eugène Delacroix in St Denis-du-Saint-Sacrement, Paris). 1866–7.
British Museum, London (Cat. No. 6).

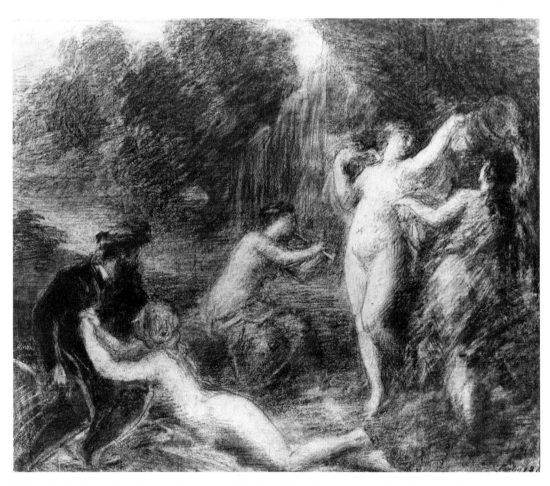

26 Henri Fantin-Latour, *Tannhäuser on the Venusberg*. 1863. City of Bristol Museum & Art Gallery (Cat. No. 25).

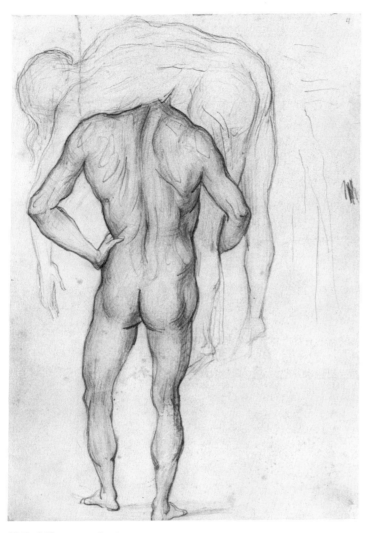

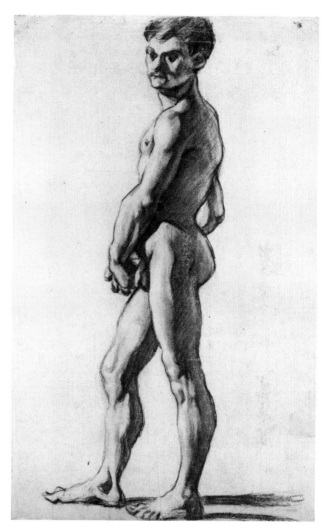

27 Paul Cézanne, *Study of a Man Seen from the Back Carrying a Body* (after a study by Luca Signorelli). 1867–70. Saltwood Castle (Cat. No. 7).

28 Paul Cézanne, *Study of a Male Nude Seen in Profile Facing Left.* 1863–6. Fitzwilliam Museum, Cambridge (Cat. No. 5).

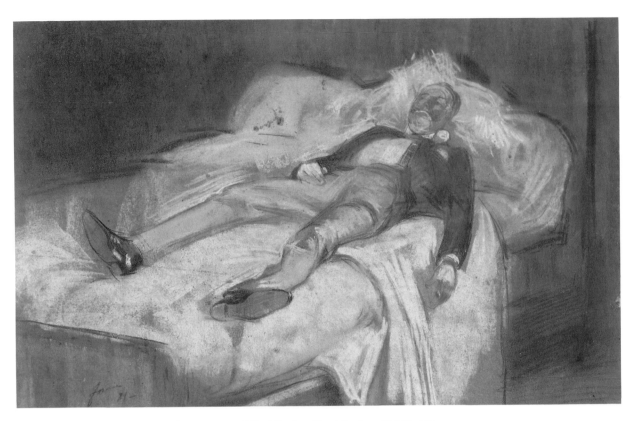

29 Jean-Louis Forain, *Man in a State of Happy Repose*. 1881. Collection of Lord Goodman (Cat. No. 27).

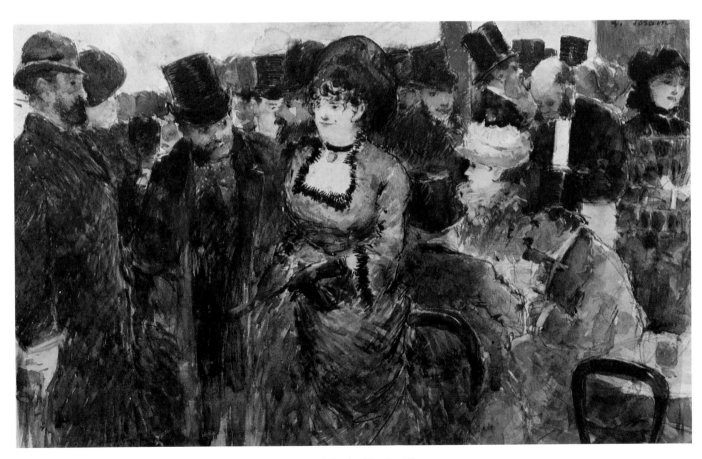

30 Jean-Louis Forain, *Theatre Foyer (Couloir de théâtre)*. *c*.1880–1. Private Collection (Cat. No. 26).

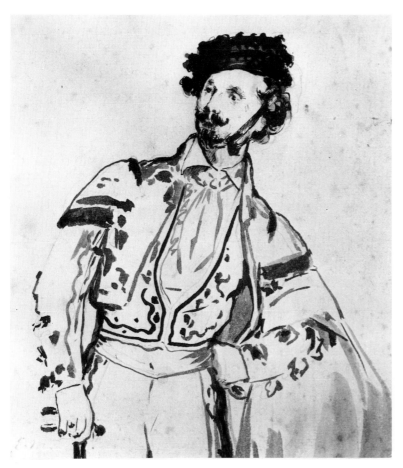

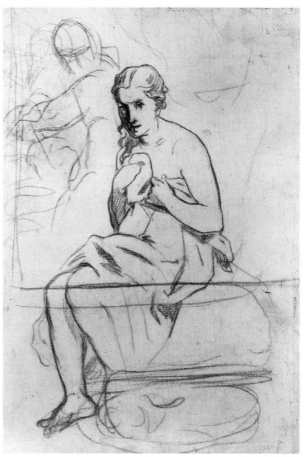

31 Édouard Manet, *Don Mariano Camprubi*. 1862. The Burrell Collection, Glasgow (Cat. No. 35).

32 Édouard Manet, *Study of a Woman at her Toilet*. 1862. Courtauld Institute Galleries (Samuel Courtauld Collection), London (Cat. No. 34).

59

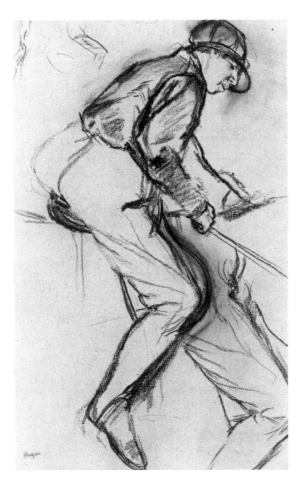 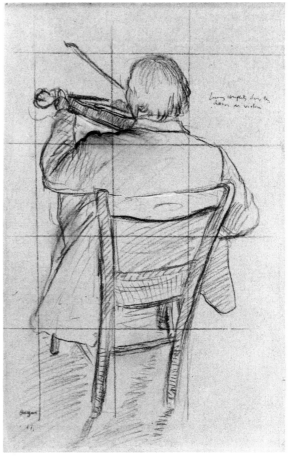

33 Edgar Degas, *Study of a Jockey. c.*1882. Ashmolean Museum, Oxford (Cat. No. 19).

34 Edgar Degas, *Study of a Violinist Seen from the Back.* 1875–6. Ashmolean Museum, Oxford (Cat. No. 15).

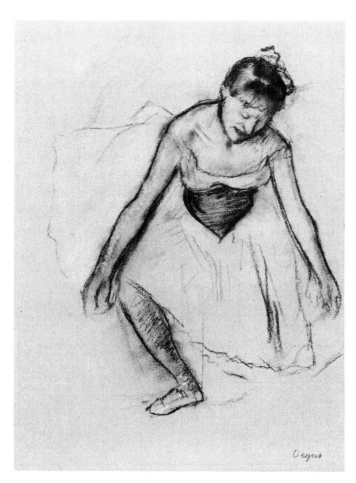

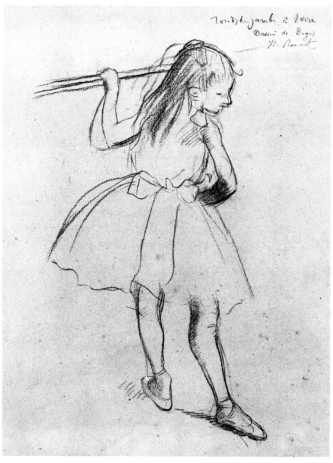

35 Edgar Degas, *Study of a Dancer Bowing. c.*1880. Plymouth City Museum &
Art Gallery (Cat. No. 18).

36 Edgar Degas, *Study of a Girl Dancer (Suzanne Mante) at the Barre (Petit rat
à la barre). c.*1878. Fitzwilliam Museum, Cambridge (Cat. No. 16).

37 Auguste Renoir, *The Snack (La Collation). c.*1895.
Fitzwilliam Museum, Cambridge (Cat. No. 72).

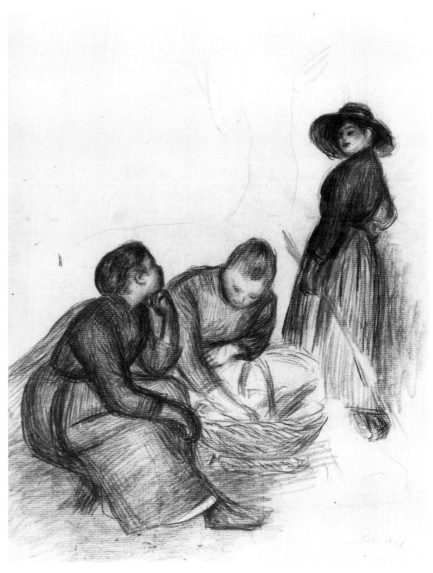

38 Léon Lhermitte, *Interior: Nine Peasant Women Seated in a Church*. 1867. Victoria and Albert Museum, London (Cat. No. 33).

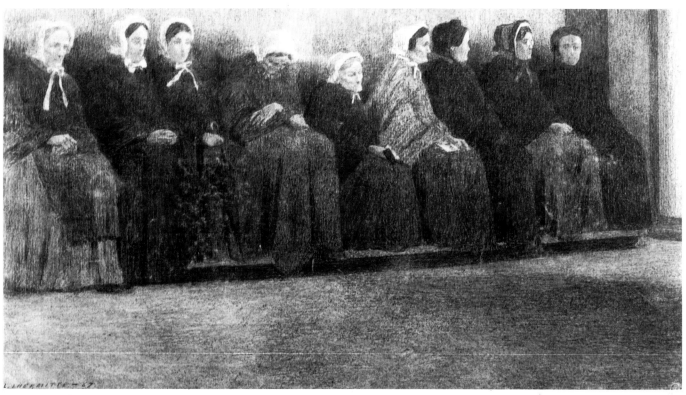

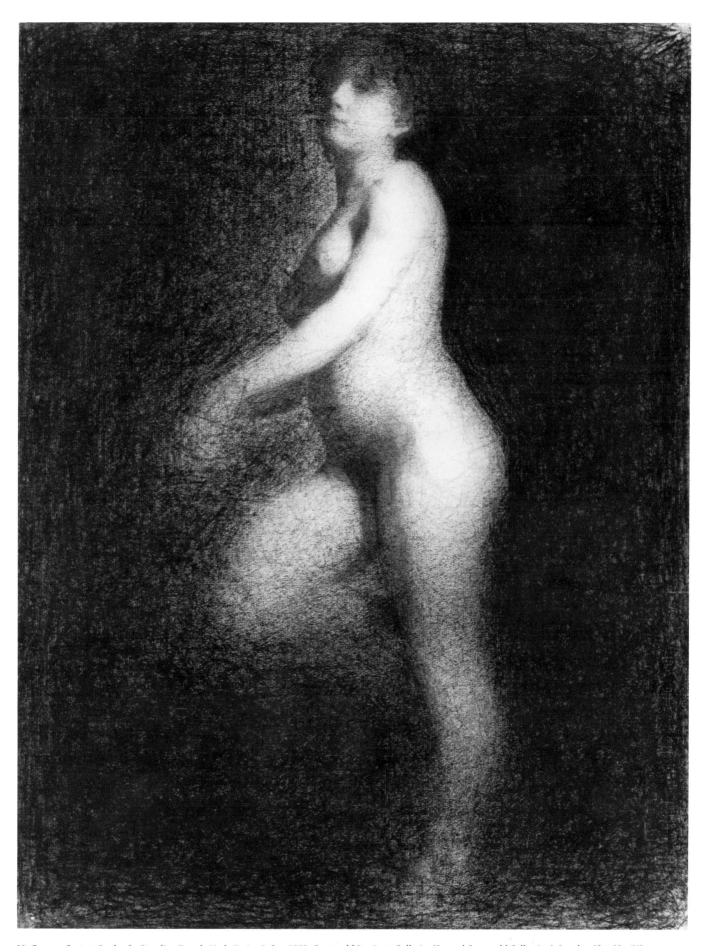

39 Georges Seurat, *Study of a Standing Female Nude Facing Left*. *c*.1879. Courtauld Institute Galleries (Samuel Courtauld Collection), London (Cat. No. 73).

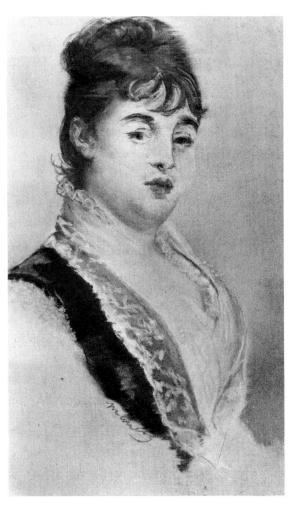

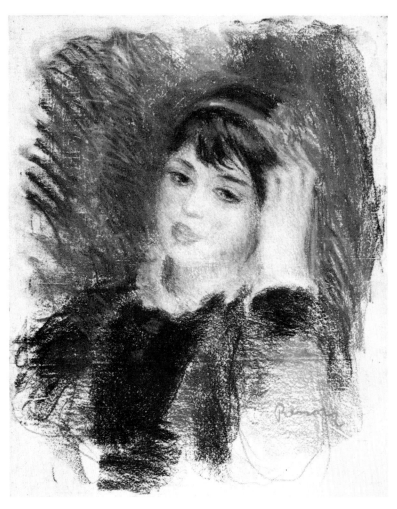

40 Édouard Manet, *Marie Colombier*. 1880. The Burrell
Collection, Glasgow (Cat. No. 41).

41 Auguste Renoir, *Head of a Young Woman*. *c*.1878–80. Anonymous loan to the
Fitzwilliam Museum, Cambridge (Cat. No. 66).

42 Alfred Sisley, *Portrait of the Artist's Son, Pierre*. 1880. Garman-Ryan Collection, Walsall Museum and Art Gallery (Cat. No. 79).

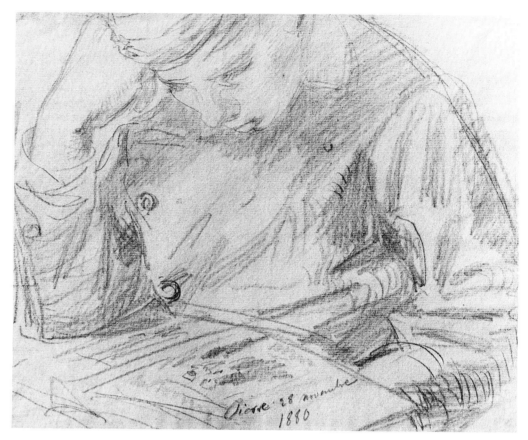

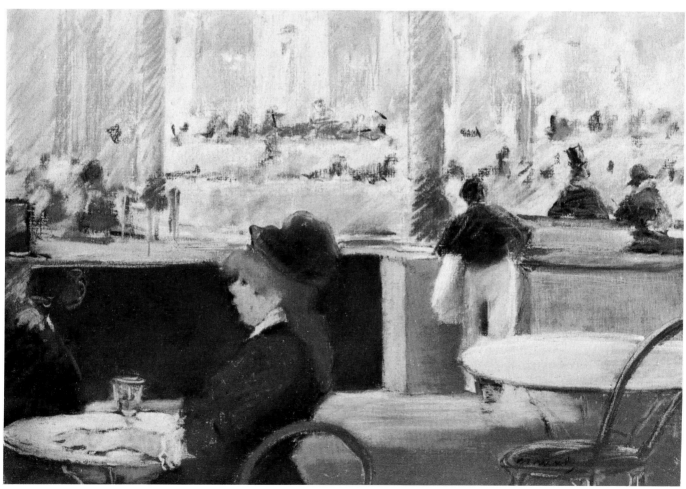

43 Édouard Manet, *A Café, Place du Théâtre-Français*. c.1877–8. The Burrell Collection, Glasgow (Cat. No. 37).

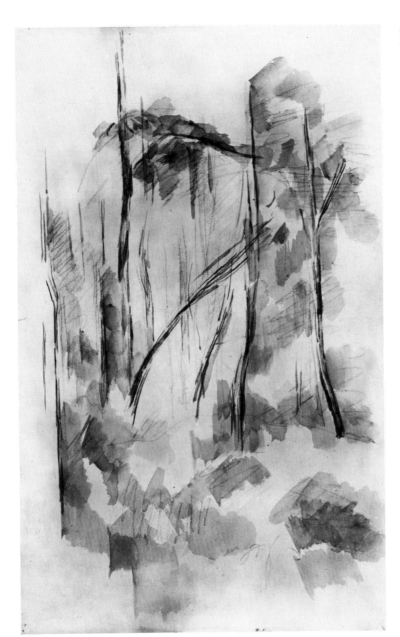

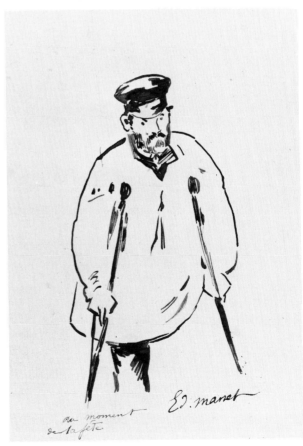

44 Paul Cézanne, *Sous-bois*. 1887–9. Victoria and Albert Museum, London (Cat. No. 11).

45 Édouard Manet, *A Man on Crutches*. 1878. Ashmolean Museum, Oxford (Cat. No. 38).

46 Camille Pissarro, *Landscape with Ploughed Field, Eragny. c.*1887–8. Ashmolean Museum, Oxford (Cat. No. 58).

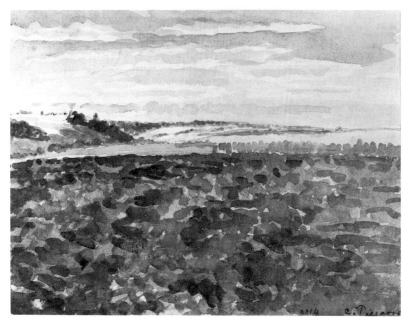

47 Armand Guillaumin, *Le Quai de Bercy.* 1867. Whitworth Art Gallery, University of Manchester (Cat. No. 30).

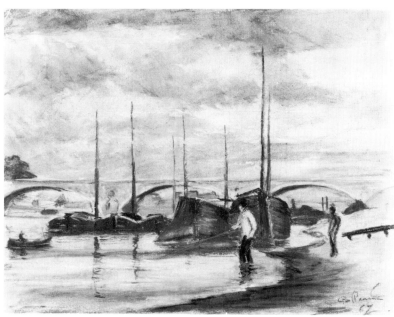

48 Camille Pissarro, *The Corn Stooks (Les Moyettes). c.*1887. Whitworth Art Gallery, University of Manchester (Cat. No. 57).

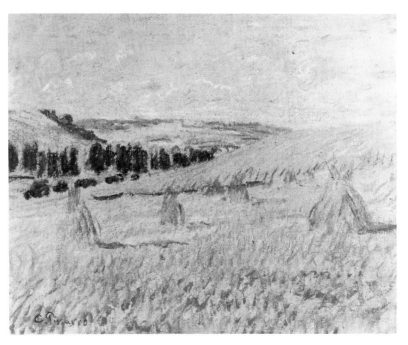

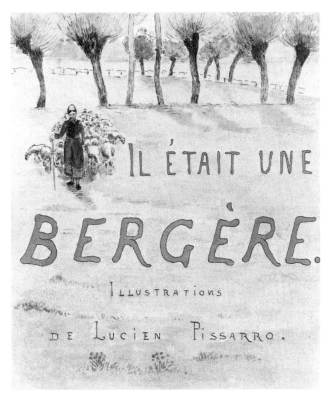

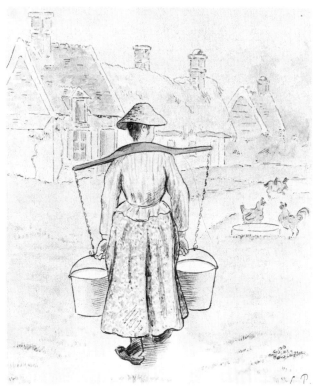

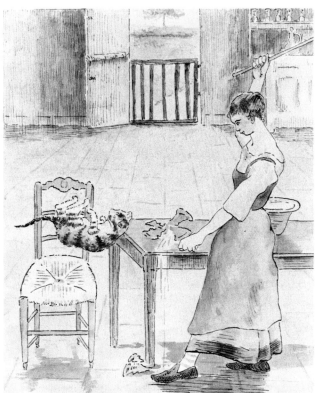

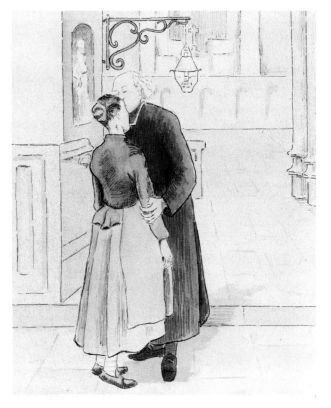

49a Lucien Pissarro, *Il était une bergère (There Once Was A Shepherdess)*; 49b *She Went to Make a Cheese*; 49c *The Shepherdess Lost her Temper*;
49d *We'll Embrace in Forgiveness. c.*1886. Ashmolean Museum, Oxford (Cat. Nos. 61a–d).

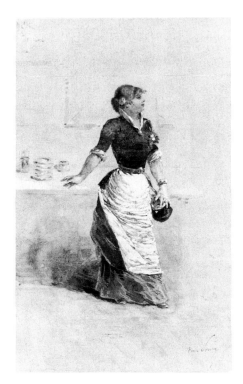

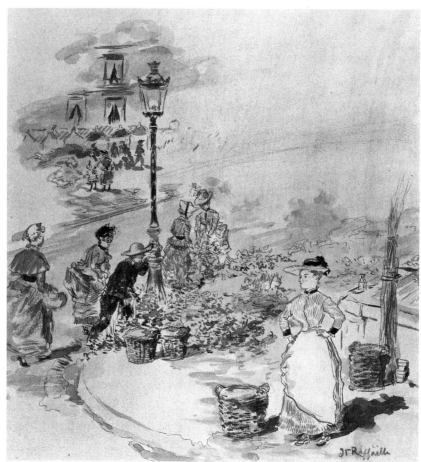

50 Henri Somm, *The Beer Waitress (La Serveuse de Bocks)*. c.1875–80. Private Collection (Cat. No. 81).

51 Jean-François Raffaëlli, *Study for 'Les Types de Paris: Les Petites Marchandes des rues'*. 1889. Private Collection (Cat. No. 64).

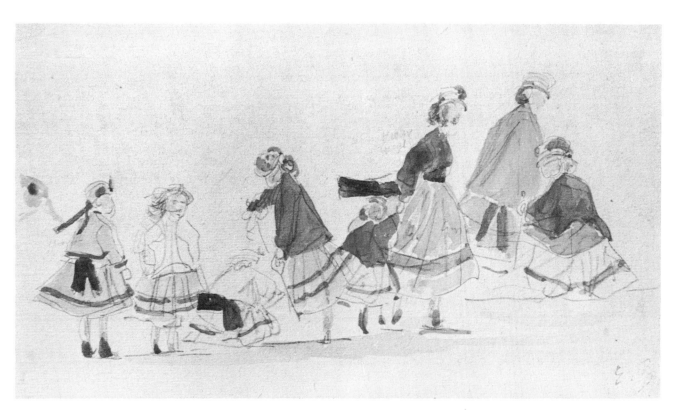

52 Louis-Eugène Boudin, *Study of Figures on the Beach*. c.1865–70. Garman-Ryan Collection, Walsall Museum and Art Gallery (Cat. No. 4).

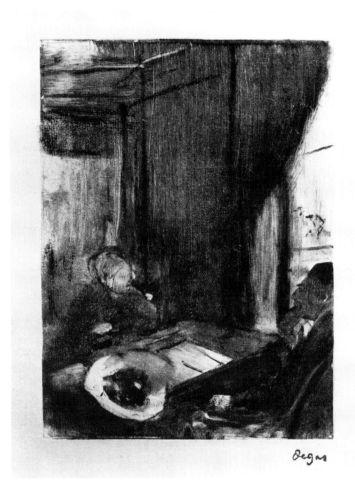

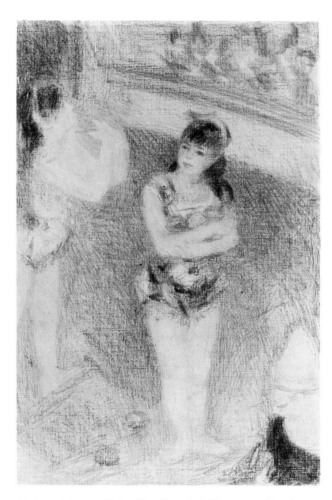

53 Edgar Degas, *Monsieur and Madame Cardinal. c.*1880. Dundee Art Galleries and Museums (Cat. No. 17).

54 Auguste Renoir, *Study of Two Circus Girls (Francisca and Angelina Wartenberg) of the Cirque Fernando.* 1879. Saltwood Castle (Cat. No. 67).

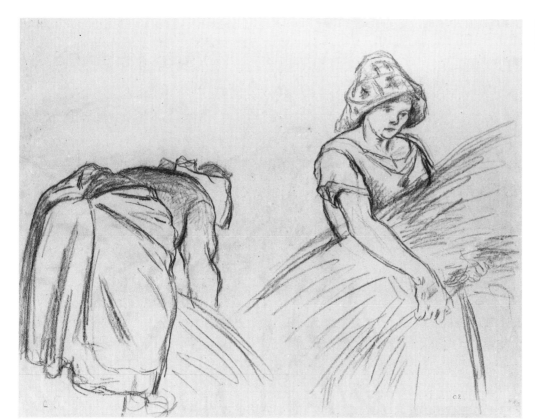

55 Camille Pissarro, *Study for 'The Harvest'. c.*1882. Ashmolean Museum, Oxford (Cat. No. 53).

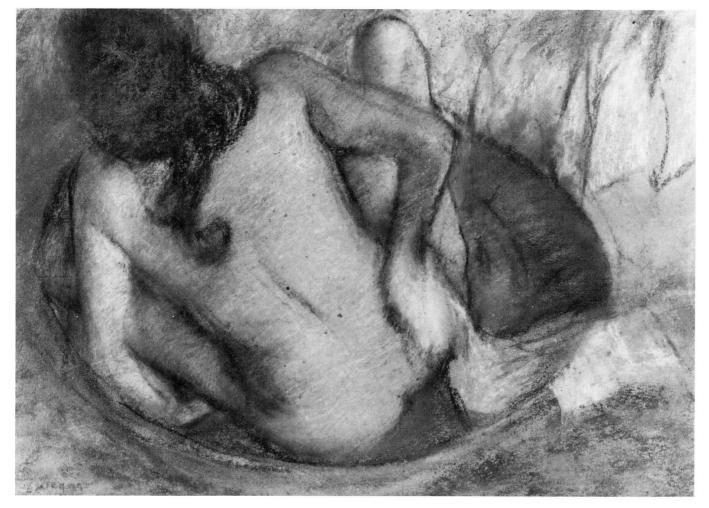

56 Edgar Degas, *Nude in a Tub (Femme au tub).* 1884. The Burrell Collection, Glasgow (Cat. No. 21).

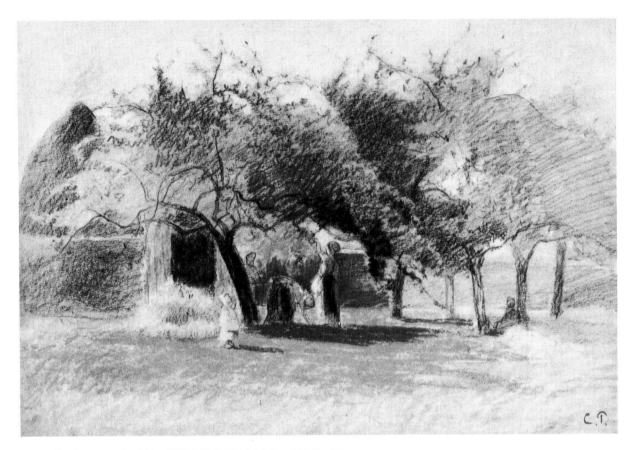

57 Camille Pissarro, *Apple-picking*. 1870–5. York City Art Gallery (Cat. No. 49).

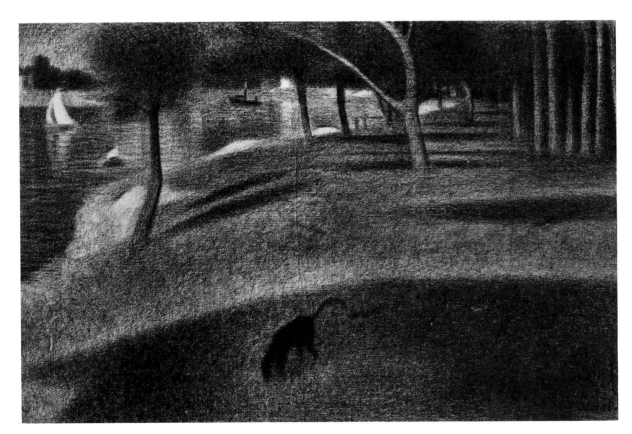

58 Georges Seurat, *Study for 'La Grande-Jatte: Landscape with Dog'*. c.1884–5. British Museum, London (Cat. No. 75).

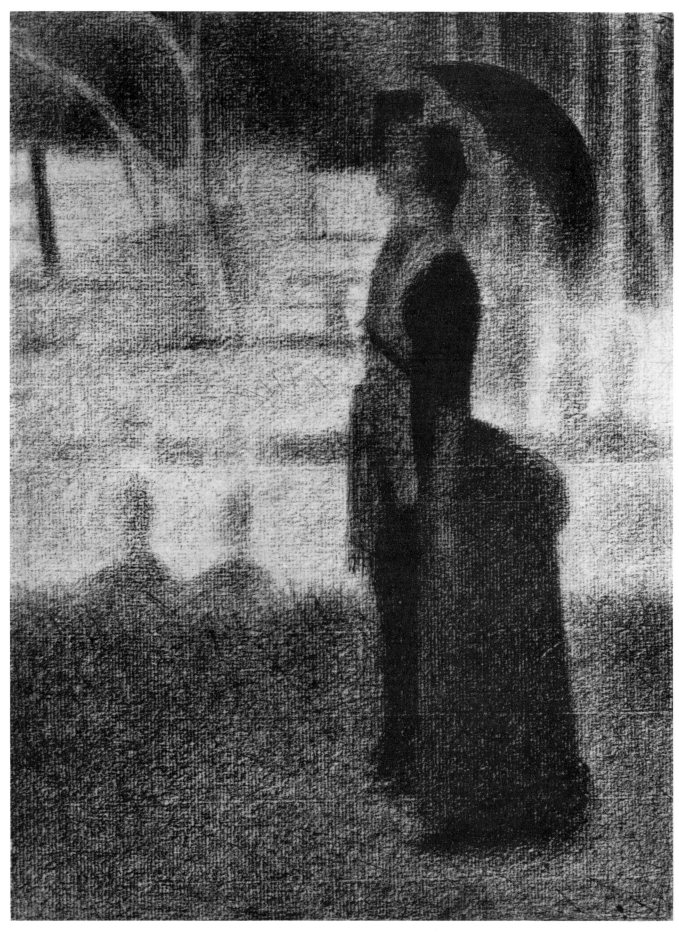

59 Georges Seurat, *Study for 'La Grande-Jatte: The Couple'*. c.1884–5. British Museum, London (Cat. No. 76).

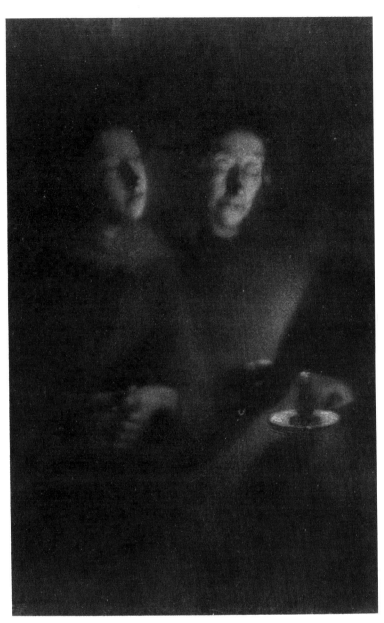

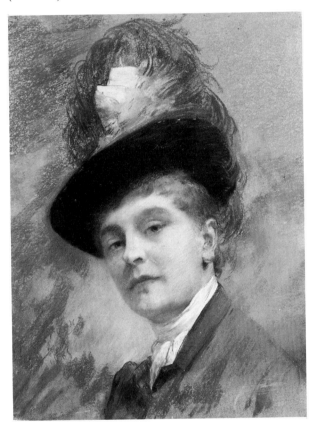

60 Charles-Albert Lebourg, *The Artist's Wife and Mother-in-Law Reading a Letter by Candlelight*. c.1879. British Museum, London (Cat. No. 32).

61 Henri Gervex, *Portrait of a Lady in a Hat*. 1885. Private Collection (Cat. No. 29).

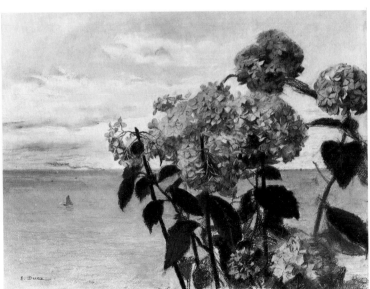

62 Ernest-Ange Duez, *Hydrangeas*. c.1888. Private Collection (Cat. No. 24).

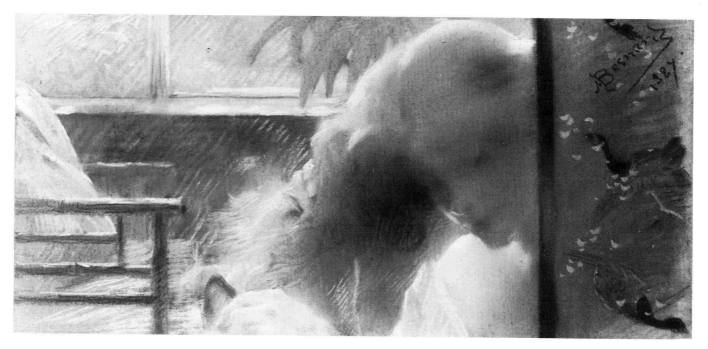

63 Paul-Albert Besnard, *The Model*. 1887. Private Collection, courtesy of Whitford and Hughes (Cat. No. 1).

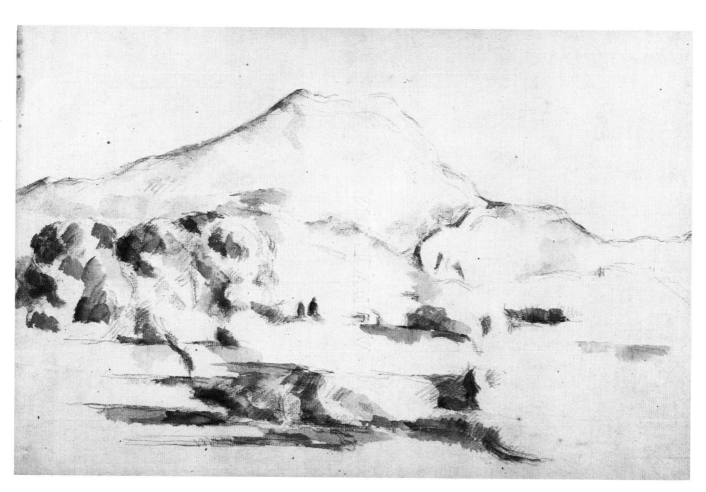

64 Paul Cézanne, *La Montagne Saint-Victoire Seen from the South-West*. 1885–7. Courtauld Institute Galleries (Samuel Courtauld Collection), London (Cat. No. 9).

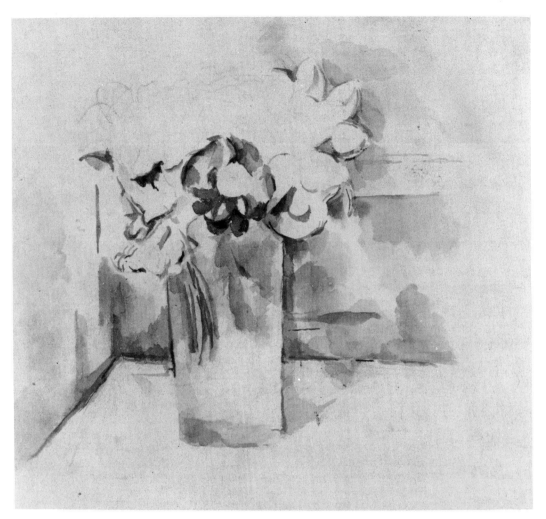

65 Paul Cézanne, *Vase of Flowers*. 1885–8 (or possibly later). Fitzwilliam Museum, Cambridge (Cat. No. 10).

66 Johan Barthold Jongkind, *Landscape near La Côte-Saint-André (Dauphiné)*. 1880. British Museum, London (Cat. No. 31).

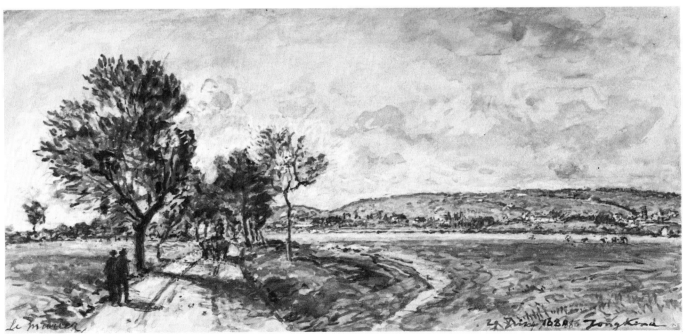

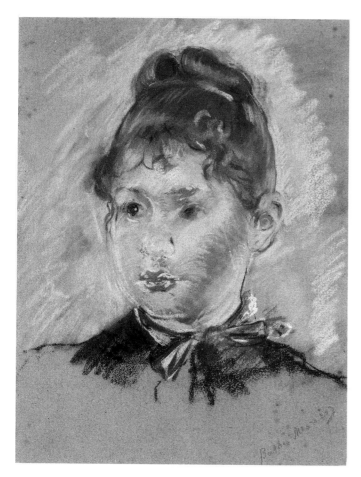

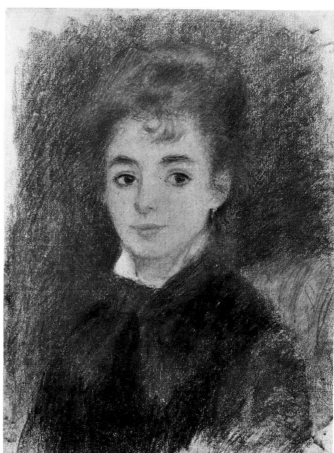

ABOVE 67 Berthe Morisot,
Isabelle. 1885. Robert and Lisa
Sainsbury Collection,
University of East Anglia (Cat.
No. 44).

ABOVE RIGHT 68 Auguste
Renoir, *Head of a Young
Woman with Red Hair*.
c.1876–8. The Burrell
Collection, Glasgow (Cat. No.
65).

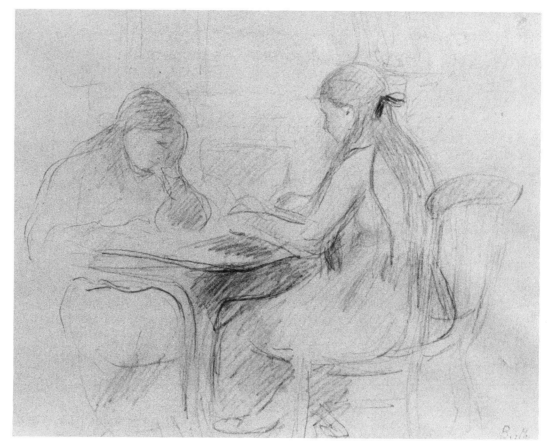

69 Berthe Morisot, *Study of
Two Girls Writing at a Table*.
c.1890. Private Collection (Cat.
No. 45).

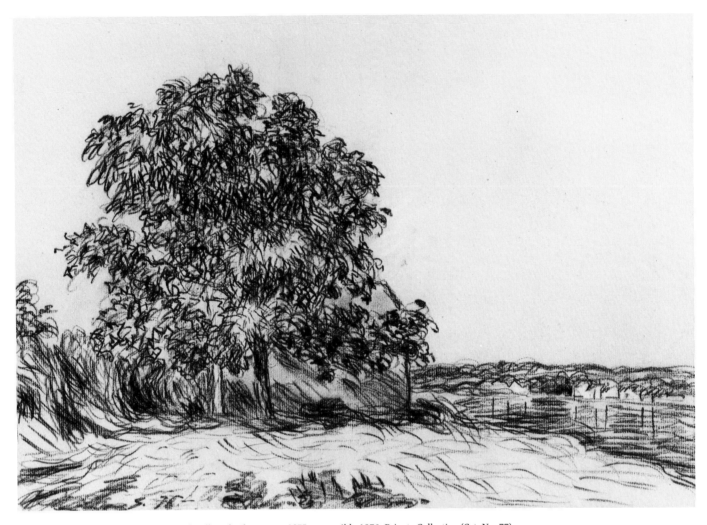

70 Alfred Sisley, *La Plaine de Thomery et le village de Champagne*. 1875, or possibly 1876. Private Collection (Cat. No. 77).

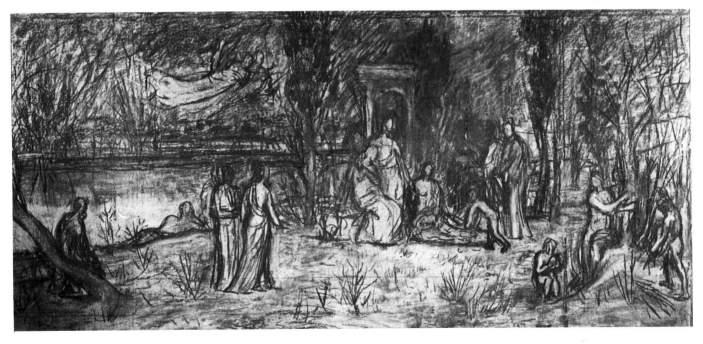

71 Pierre Puvis de Chavannes, *Study for 'The Sacred Grove' (Le Bois sacré)*. *c*.1882–4. Garman-Ryan Collection, Walsall Museum and Art Gallery (Cat. No. 63).

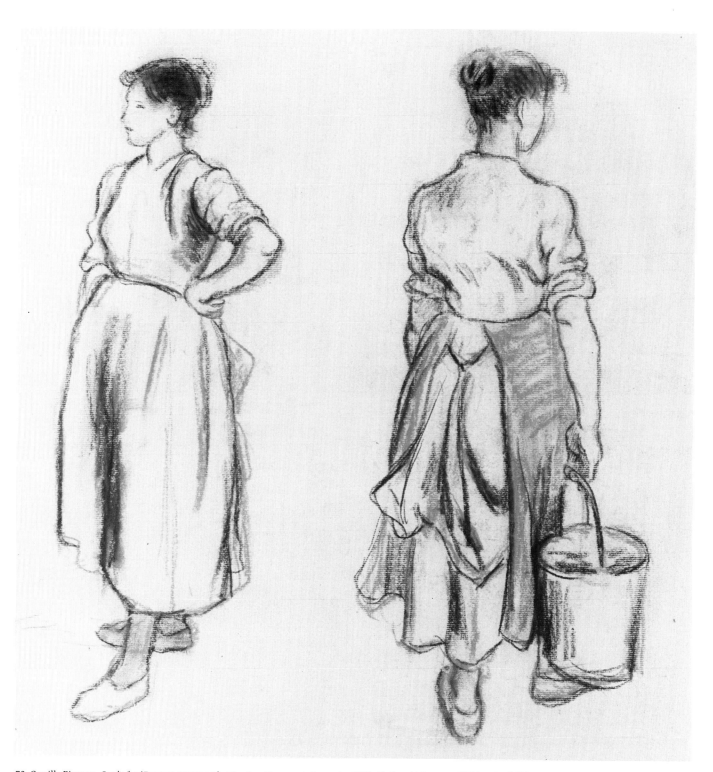

72 Camille Pissarro, *Study for 'Peasant Women Chatting in a Farmyard, Eragny'. c.*1895. National Museum of Wales, Cardiff (Cat. No. 60).

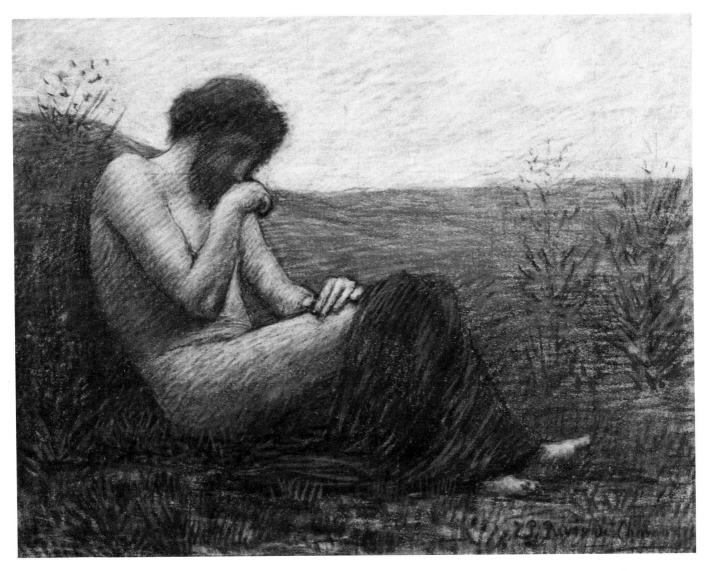

73 Pierre Puvis de Chavannes,
*Solitude. c.*1879–83. Whitworth Art
Gallery, University of Manchester
(Cat. No. 62).

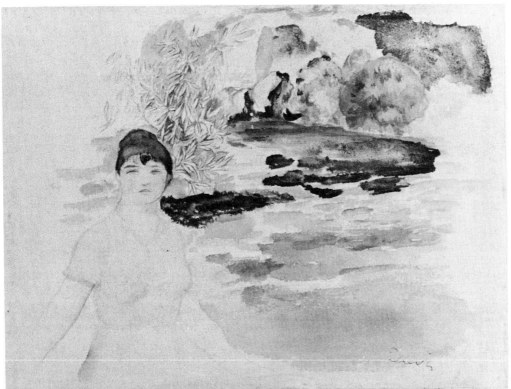

74 Auguste Renoir, *Young Woman
by a Lake. c.*1885. Ashmolean
Museum, Oxford (Cat. No. 69).

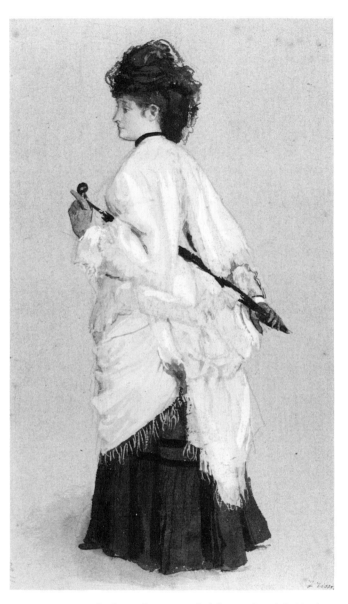

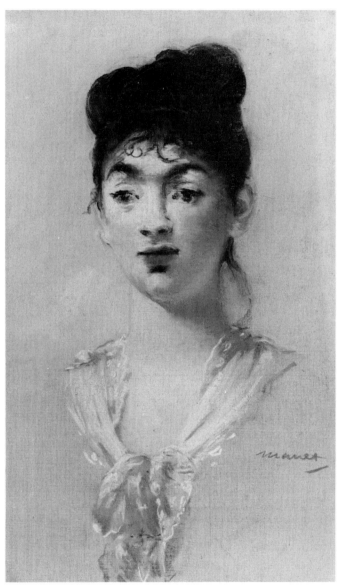

75 James Tissot, *Study of a Standing Woman for 'The Captain and the Mate'*. *c*.1873. Ashmolean Museum, Oxford (Cat. No. 82).

76 Édouard Manet, *Mlle Suzette Lemaire, full face. c*.1880. Private Collection (Cat. No. 40).

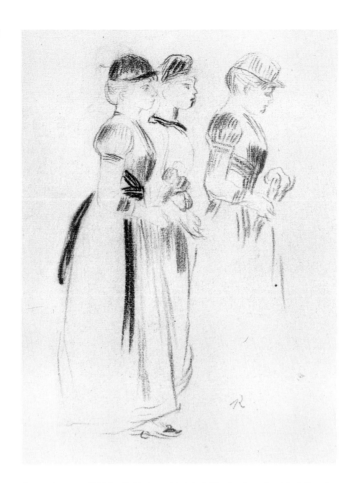

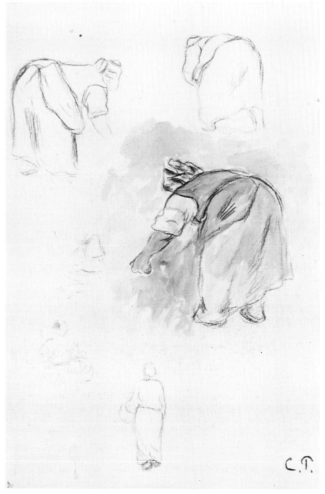

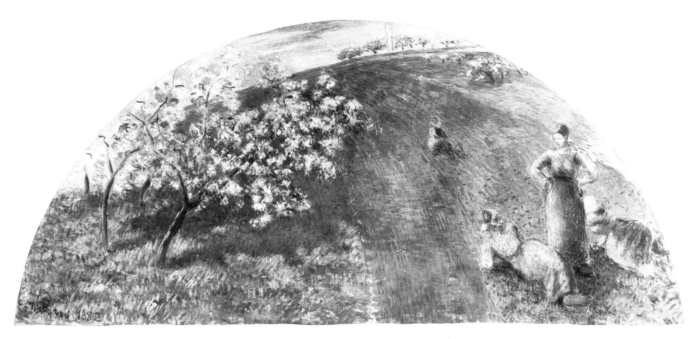

79 Camille Pissarro, *Spring: Peasant Women in a Field*. 1882. Collection of Mr and Mrs Julian Sofaer (Cat. No. 54).

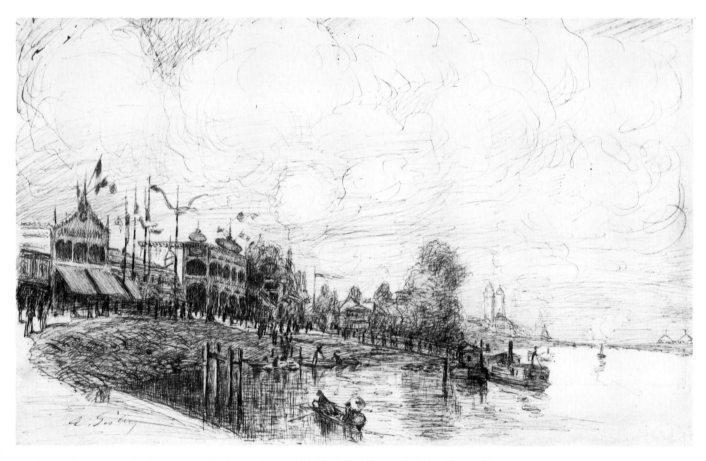

80 Alfred Sisley, *Drawing after 'La Seine au Point du Jour, fête du 30 juin 1878'*. 1878. Private Collection (Cat. No. 78).

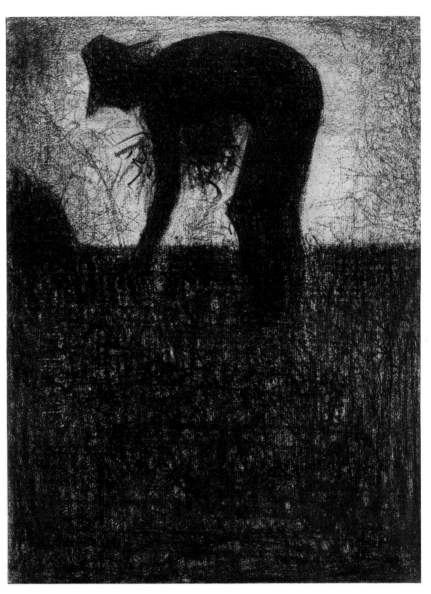

81 Georges Seurat, *The Gleaner*.
*c.*1882. British Museum, London
(Cat. No. 74).

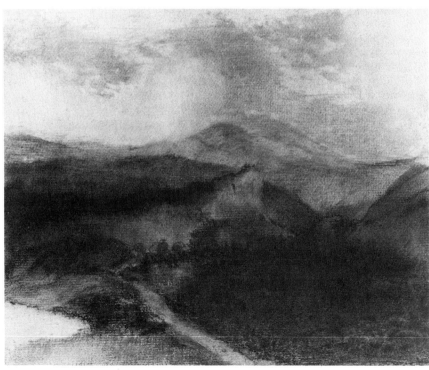

84

82 Edgar Degas, *Landscape
(Paysage)*. *c.*1890–3. Private
Collection (Cat. No. 23).

Catalogue

The entries in this Catalogue are not intended to be comprehensive. The Literature and Exhibition sections in particular are selective though they do contain all the essential items, and the reader is advised to consult these for further bibliographical information.

PAUL-ALBERT BESNARD (1849–1934)

Born in Paris. Pupil of Cabanel at the École des Beaux-Arts. Won the Grand Prix de Rome, 1874. Influenced by the Impressionists, but never exhibited with them. Degas once remarked that 'Besnard is flying with our wings'. Travelled to England, 1879–83, and later to North Africa and India. First exhibited at the Salon, 1868, and became renowned as a portraitist and painter of large decorative schemes. Also a considerable printmaker and critic.

1. **The Model.** 1887. Plate 63.
   Pastel on brown board. 37 × 77 cm.
   Signed and dated upper right:
   'A. Besnard/1887'.
   PROV: France, private collection; London, Whitford and Hughes.
   Private Collection, courtesy of Whitford and Hughes.

LOUIS-EUGÈNE BOUDIN (1824–98)

Born at Honfleur. Lived mainly in Le Havre, but travelled extensively along the coasts of Holland and France. Influenced by Troyon and Millet. Established himself as a landscape and marine painter often portraying Trouville and Deauville. Exhibited at the first Impressionist exhibition only, 1874. Friend of Jongkind and Courbet.

2. **Sunset over the Sea.** 1860–70.
   Plate 23.
   Pastel on brown paper. 17.1 × 28.1 cm.
   Stamp in lower corners: 'EB' (Lugt 828).
   PROV: Paris, Eugène Gourdot; London, Goupil Gallery; Seaford (Sussex), F. Hindley Smith, by whom bequeathed, 1939 (inv. PD 2380). EXH: *Cent Dessins Français*, 1976, no. 8.
   RELATED WORKS: *Study of the Sky at Sunset*, pastel on beige/pink paper (Paris, Louvre, Cabinet des Dessins, inv. RF. 4029; *Boudin. Aquarelles et Pastels*, 1965, no. 100). Also see Gottlieb, 1968, pp. 400–1.
   Lent by the Syndics of the Fitzwilliam Museum, Cambridge.

3. **The Beach at Trouville with the Hôtel des Roches-Noires in the Background.** 1860–5. Plate 16.
   Pastel. 18.5 × 29.5 cm. Signed.
   RELATED WORKS: Schmit, nos. 261 (c.1862–5), 273 (1863) and 293 (1864). The motif was painted three times by Monet in 1870 (Wildenstein, 1974, nos. 155–7).
   Private Collection.

4. **Study of Figures on the Beach.**
   c.1865–70. Plate 52.
   Watercolour and pencil. 14 × 24 cm.
   Stamp: lower right: 'E.B.' (Lugt 828).
   PROV: Lady Kathleen Epstein/Sally Ryan, by whom presented, 1973 (GR. 8). LIT: Vigurs, 1976, pp. 20–1.
   RELATED WORKS: for this type of drawing see Gottlieb, 1968, pp. 399–401.
   Lent by the Garman-Ryan Collection, Walsall Museum and Art Gallery.

PAUL CÉZANNE (1839–1906)

Born at Aix-en-Provence, where he at first studied law. Amongst early influences were Delacroix and Manet. Exhibited Salon des Refusés, 1863, and at two of the Impressionist exhibitions, 1874 and 1877. In mid-1870s encouraged by Pissarro as landscape painter. From mid-1880s until his death tended to work alone mainly in Provence. Increasing reputation among young painters from late 1880s, although his work was not widely known until the one-man exhibition organized by Ambroise Vollard in Paris in 1895. Painted landscape, still-lifes, portraits and figure subjects, all of which exerted a profound influence on the development of twentieth-century art.

5. **Study of a Male Nude Seen in Profile Facing Left.** 1863–6. Plate 28.
   Charcoal heightened with white.
   49.3 × 30.8 cm.
   PROV: Paris, Vignier; Cambridge, Louis C. G. Clarke, by whom bequeathed, 1960 (inv. PD. 55-1961). LIT: Chappuis, 1973, no. 99. EXH: *Watercolour and Pencil Drawings by Cézanne*, 1973, no. 2; *Cent Dessins Français*, 1976, no. 12; *Drawings from the Collection of Louis C. G. Clarke*, 1981–2, pp. 78–9.
   RELATED WORKS: Chappuis, 1973, nos. 97–8.

For use of the same model, see Chappuis, 1973, nos. 93, 104–6, 108–12 and *Study of a Male Nude Sitting on the Ground*, 1863–6, charcoal (Christie's, 28 November 1972, no. 52).
Lent by the Syndics of the Fitzwilliam Museum, Cambridge.

6. **The Entombment** (after the painting by Eugène Delacroix in St Denis-du-Saint-Sacrament, Paris). 1866–7. Plate 25.
   Pencil. 18 × 24 cm. Verso: *Sheet of Studies (including a study after the painting 'Apollo Vanquishing the Serpent Python' by Delacroix in the Galerie d'Apollon, Palais du Louvre)*. Pencil.
   PROV: Paris, Cézanne fils; Paris, Paul Guillaume; London, Kenneth Clark; Oxford, Michael Sadleir; London, F. A. Drey. LIT: Chappuis, 1973, no. 167 (verso, no. 180); Lichtenstein, 1975, p. 118; Ballas, 1981, p. 224.
   RELATED WORKS: *The Entombment*, wood engraving after Delacroix published in *L'Artiste*, 2 February 1845, p. 80 and *Apollo Vanquishing the Serpent Python*, wood engraving after Delacroix published in *L'Illustration*, 27 December 1851, p. 408.
   Lent by the Trustees of the British Museum, London.

7. **Study of a Man Seen from the back Carrying a Body** (after a study by Luca Signorelli for the frescoes in the Cappella di S. Brizio, Duomo, Orvieto). 1867–70. Plate 27.
   Pencil and red crayon. 24 × 18 cm.
   Verso: *Study for 'L'Éternel féminin'*. Pencil.
   PROV: London, Kenneth Clark. LIT: Reff, 1960, pp. 304 and 306; Chappuis, 1973, no. 182 (verso no. 257). EXH: *Watercolour and Pencil Drawings by Cézanne*, 1973, no. 5.
   RELATED WORKS: Luca Signorelli, *Study of a Man Seen from the back Carrying a Body*, point of the brush with brown ink heightened with white on a grey-green prepared ground (Paris, Louvre, Cabinet des Dessins). Other copies of this drawing by Cézanne are Chappuis, 1973, nos. 488, of

1879–82, and 675, of 1883–6.
Lent from Saltwood Castle.

8. Three Female Bathers. 1874–5. Plate 8.
Pencil, watercolour and gouache.
11.4 × 12.7 cm.
PROV: Paris, Ambroise Vollard; Orrony,
P. Hazard (Paris, 1–3 December 1919, no.
258); Paris, Bernheim Jeune; Gregynog
Hall, Montgomeryshire, Gwendoline and
Margaret Davies, by whom bequeathed,
1963. LIT: V. 898; Ingamells, 1967, no. 34(b)
p. 83; Rewald, 1983, no. 62. EXH: (?)Paris,
Ambroise Vollard, 1895; *Watercolour and
Pencil Drawings by Cézanne*, 1973, no. 23;
Paul Cézanne Aquarelle, 1982, no. 109.
RELATED WORKS: *Trois baigneuses*, oil,
1875–7 (Paris, Musée d'Orsay; V. 266 and
Gache-Patin, 1984, p. 140).
Lent by the National Museum of Wales,
Cardiff.

**9. La Montagne Saint-Victoire Seen
from the South-West.** 1885–7. Plate 64.
Pencil and watercolour or dilute
gouache on off-white paper.
32.8 × 50.5 cm (uneven).
PROV: Paris, Paul Cézanne *fils*; Paris,
Bernheim Jeune, 1904; Lausanne, Gottlieb
Friedrich Reber; London, P. M. Turner;
London, Samuel Courtauld, 1929, by whom
presented, 1932. LIT: V. 1023; Cooper,
1954, no. 110, pp. 133–4; Rewald, 1983, no.
279. EXH: *Watercolour and Pencil Drawings
by Cézanne*, 1973, no. 55; *Mantegna to
Cézanne*, 1983, no. 100; *The Impressionists
and the Post-Impressionists from The
Courtauld Collection*, 1984, no. 17.
Lent by the Courtauld Institute Galleries
(Samuel Courtauld Collection).

10. Vase of Flowers. 1885–8 (or possibly
later). Plate 65.
Pencil and watercolour. 46.6 × 30 cm.
Verso: *Clearing in a Wood*. Pencil and
watercolour.
PROV: Paris, Ambroise Vollard; London, Sir
Victor Schuster; London, McNeill Reid;
London, Reid & Lefevre; Cambridge,
Captain S. W. Sykes, by whom bequeathed
(PD. 6-1966). LIT: Rewald, 1983, no. 223
(verso no. 300). EXH: *Watercolour and Pencil
Drawings by Cézanne*, 1973, no. 73; *Cent
Dessins Français*, 1976, no. 13; *European
Drawings from the Fitzwilliam*, 1976–7, no.
98; *Paul Cézanne Aquarelle*, 1982, no. 87.
Lent by the Syndics of the Fitzwilliam
Museum, Cambridge.

11. Sous-bois. 1887–9. Plate 44.
Pencil and watercolour. 49.6 × 32 cm.
PROV: Paris, Ambroise Vollard; Paris,
Vollard estate; Paris, Robert de Galéa;
Paris, Martin Fabiani; Geneva, Galerie
Moos (Geneva, 10 March 1951); London,
Arthur Tooth & Sons; Zürich, Fritz Nathan.
LIT: V. 1621; Wadley, 1973, p. 831;
Rewald, 1983, no. 311; Lambert, 1984, no.
XIX. EXH: *Watercolour and Pencil Drawings
by Cézanne*, 1973, no. 61; *Paul Cézanne
Aquarelle*, 1982, no. 42.
RELATED WORKS: verso of no. 10 in the
present exhibition (Rewald, 1983, no. 300).
Lent by the Victoria and Albert Museum,
London.

12. L'Homme à la pipe. 1892–6. Plate 7.
Watercolour. 48.6 × 32.7 cm. Verso:
Study of a Man's Head. Pencil.
PROV: Paris, Ambroise Vollard; Paris,
Adrien Chappuis; Paris, Paul Rosenberg;
Amsterdam, Paul Cassirer; Haarlem, Franz

Koenigs; Holland, private collection;
Switzerland, private collection. LIT: V.
1088; Chappuis, 1973, no. 1095 (verso
only); Rewald 1983, no. 378. EXH: *Paul
Cézanne Aquarelle*, 1982, no. 98; *Paper*,
1985, pp. 20–1.
RELATED WORKS: *Les Joueurs de cartes*, oil,
1892–6, V. 556, V. 557 (London, Courtauld
Institute Galleries; Cooper, 1954, no. 14), V.
558 (Paris, Musée d'Orsay); *L'Homme à la
pipe*, oil, 1892–6, V. 564 (London,
Courtauld Institute Galleries; Cooper, 1954,
no. 15); V. 566, *L'Homme à la pipe*, oil,
1892–6.
Lent by Thomas Gibson Fine Art—agent
for Owner.

HILAIRE-GERMAIN-EDGAR DEGAS
(1834–1917)

Born in Paris, but family connections with
Italy and New Orleans. Pupil of Lamothe
and a keen admirer of Ingres. Began as a
painter of historical scenes, but later concentrated upon subjects inspired by contemporary life. Opposed *plein-air* approach
to painting adopted above all by Monet.
Important also as printmaker and sculptor:
all aspects of his work reveal considerable
powers of technical experimentation.
Exhibited at seven of the Impressionist
exhibitions (missed 1882). Notorious for his
acerbic wit. Suffered during later years
from failing eyesight.

**13. Venus (after a figure from the
painting 'Pallas Expelling the Vices'
by Andrea Mantegna).** c.1855. Plate
20. Pencil. 29.1 × 20.2 cm. Stamp lower
left: 'Degas' (Lugt 658).
PROV: Atelier Degas, Vente IV, Paris, 2–4
July 1919, no. 125c; London, Dr Grete
Ring, by whom bequeathed, 1954. LIT:
Pickvance, 1964, p. 83. EXH: *Degas, Pastels
and Drawings*, 1969, no. 4; *Edgar Degas
1834–1917*, 1983, no. 3; *Degas e l'Italia*,
1984–5, no. 8.
RELATED WORKS: *Partial copies after
Mantegna's 'Pallas Expelling the Vices'*,
pencil, 1859, in Notebook 14, pp. 7–8
(Paris, Bibliothèque Nationale; Reff, Vol. I,
1976, p. 83). *Copy after Mantegna's 'Pallas
Expelling the Vices'*, charcoal and pastel on
toned canvas, 1897 (Paris, Louvre, Cabinet
des Dessins; L. Supplement, 144).
Lent by the Visitors of The Ashmolean
Museum, Oxford.

**14. Studies for 'St John the Baptist and
the Angel'.** 1856–8. Plate 19.
Pencil with pen and brown ink.
38.3 × 25.8 cm. Inscribed lower right:
'Rome'.
PROV: Nice, Mlle Jeanne Fèvre, the artist's
niece (Paris, 12 June 1934, no. 37); London,
Dr Grete Ring, by whom bequeathed, 1954.
LIT: Nathanson and Olszewski, 1980, p.
250. EXH: *Degas, Pastels and Drawings*,
1969, no. 6; *Degas e l'Italia*, 1984–5, no. 33.
RELATED WORKS: *St John the Baptist and the
Angel*, watercolour, 1856–8 (L. 20) and *St
John the Baptist*, oil, 1856–8 (L. 21). For
related drawings see Nathanson and
Olszewski, 1980.
Lent by the Visitors of The Ashmolean
Museum, Oxford.

**15. Study of a Violinist Seen from the
Back.** 1875–6. Plate 34.
Charcoal heightened with white chalk
on grey paper. Squared. 47.9 × 31.2 cm.
Inscribed upper right: 'lueurs et reflets

sur le dessous du violon'. Stamp lower
left: 'Degas' (Lugt 658).
PROV: Atelier Degas, Vente III, Paris, 7–9
April 1919, no. 157(1); Paris, Jacques
Dubourg; London, Agnew, 1937; Oswald
T. Falk, 1937; Oxford, John Bryson, by
whom bequeathed, 1977. LIT: under L. 399;
Browse, 1949, p. 349, pl. 36a; Wick, 1959,
p. 92; Lloyd, 1978, p. 285. EXH: *Degas,
1879*, 1979, no. 24; *Dürer to Cézanne*,
1982–3, no. 108; *Edgar Degas 1834–1917*,
1983, no. 10.
RELATED WORKS: *The Rehearsal*, tempera,
1875–6 (Shelburne Museum of Art,
Shelburne, Vermont; L. 399). Other preparatory studies as listed by Lemoisne: L.
379; Atelier Degas, Vente II, 11–13
December 1918, nos. 277 and 347; Atelier
Degas, Vente III, 7–9 April 1919, nos. 326,
343, 357(2) and 359(2). To these can be
added Atelier Degas, Vente IV, 2–4 July
1919, no. 265a.
Lent by the Visitors of The Ashmolean
Museum, Oxford.

**16. Study of a Girl Dancer (Suzanne
Mante) at the Barre (Petit rat à la
barre).** c.1878. Plate 36.
Black chalk on pink paper.
34.1 × 24.1 cm. Inscribed upper right:
'ronds de jambe à terre' and in a
different hand, presumably that of
Henri Rouart, 'Dessin de Degas H.
Rouart'.
PROV: Paris, Henri Rouart; Christie's, 12
June 1914, no. 96, bt. Agnew; Cambridge,
Louis C. G. Clarke; Cambridge, Andrew
Gow, 1961, by whom bequeathed through
the National Art-Collections Fund, 1978
(PD. 33-1978). LIT: Browse, 1949, p. 364, pl.
78; Millet, 1979, p. 112. EXH: *Andrew
Gow Bequest*, 1978, no. 16; *Selected Works from
the Gow Bequest*, 1978, no. 27; *Drawings
from the Collection of Louis C. G. Clarke*,
1981–2, pp. 77–8.
RELATED WORKS: Browse, 1949, pls. 76, and
77 (New York, Metropolitan Museum of
Art, inv. 29-100.943); Minneapolis
Institute of Arts (inv. 26.10; see *Degas.
Pastelle, Ölskizzen, Zeichnungen*, 1984, No.
115).
Lent by the Syndics of the Fitzwilliam
Museum, Cambridge.

17. Monsieur and Madame Cardinal.
c.1880. Plate 53.
Monotype in black ink with touches of
charcoal. 21.2 × 15.9 cm. Stamp lower
right: 'Degas' (Lugt 658).
EXH: *Degas, 1879*, 1979, no. 82, repr.
RELATED WORKS: *M. Cardinal about to Write
a Letter*, monotype, c.1880 (*Degas
Monotypes*, 1968, no. 202, repr.); pencil
sketches in Notebook 27, pp. 3, 4, 6 (Paris,
Bibliothèque Nationale; Reff, 1976, I, pp.
126–7).
Lent by the Dundee Art Galleries and
Museums.

18. Study of a Dancer Bowing. c.1880.
Plate 35.
Charcoal with pastel on beige paper.
Signed lower right: 'Degas'. 60 × 45 cm.
PROV: sold anonymously, Paris, 28
December 1917; London, Leicester
Galleries; A. de Pass, by whom be-
queathed, 1926. LIT: L. 612; Browse, 1949,
p. 392, pl. 169a.
RELATED WORKS: *Le Ballet vu d'une loge*,
pastel, c.1880 (L. 586) and *Trois danseuses*,
pastel, c.1882 (L. 701).

Lent by Plymouth City Museum & Art Gallery.

19. Study of a Jockey. *c.*1882. Plate 33.
Charcoal on discoloured grey paper.
50 × 32.5 cm. Stamp lower left: 'Degas' (Lugt 658).
PROV: Atelier Degas, Vente III, Paris, 7–9 April 1919, no. 98(2); London, P. M. Turner; Oxford, J. N. Bryson, by whom bequeathed, 1977. LIT: Lemoisne, 1954, p. 185, repr.; Lloyd, 1978, p. 285. EXH: *Drawings by Degas*, 1966, no. 102; *Degas 1879*, 1979, no. 14; *Dürer to Cézanne*, 1982–3, no. 109.
RELATED WORKS: *Les Courses*, pastel, *c.*1882 (L. 850); *Le Départ d'une course (derrière la barrière)*, pastel, *c.*1882 (L. 889).
Lent by the Visitors of The Ashmolean Museum, Oxford.

20. Jockeys in the Rain. *c.*1883–6. Plate 12.
Pastel. 46.9 × 63.5 cm. Signed lower left: 'degas'.
PROV: Paris, Charles B.; Étienne Bignou; London, Reid and Lefevre; Leonard Gow (Christie's, 28 May 1937, no. 23); Sir William Burrell; Glasgow, Burrell Collection (35/241). LIT: L. 646, repr. EXH: *Degas, 1879*, 1979, no. 12, repr.
RELATED WORKS: *Racecourse Scene*, oil, *c.*1868 (Montgomery, Alabama, Weil Brothers-Cotton Inc.; L. 184); *Jockeys before the Start*, mixed media, *c.*1879 (Birmingham, Barber Institute of Fine Arts; L. 649). For related drawings see *Degas, 1879*, pp. 12–15.
Lent by The Burrell Collection, Glasgow Museums and Art Galleries.

21. Nude in a Tub (Femme au tub). 1884. Plate 56.
Charcoal and pastel on grey paper.
45 × 65 cm. Signed and dated lower left: 'Degas/1884'.
PROV: Atelier Degas, Vente I, Paris, 6–8 May 1918, no. 124, repr. (10,000 francs); Nice, Mlle Jeanne Fèvre, the artist's niece (Paris, 12 June 1934, no. 95, repr.); London, Thomas Agnew and Sons; Paris, Mouradian and Vallotton; Sir William Burrell; Glasgow, Burrell Collection (35/235). LIT: Geffroy, 1886; Fénéon, *La Vogue*, 13–20, July 1886 (Fénéon, 1970, I, p. 30); Huysmans, *Certains*, 1889 (Huysmans, 1929, X, p. 23); L. 765, repr.; Pickvance, 1966, p. 19, fig. 5. EXH: *8ᵉ Exposition de la Peinture*, Paris, 1886, 'Suite de nuds' (sic).
Lent by The Burrell Collection, Glasgow Museums and Art Galleries.

22. Portrait of a Seated Woman. *c.*1885. Plate 4.
Charcoal and pastel on buff paper.
63.8 × 49.5 cm. Stamp lower left: 'Degas' (Lugt 658).
PROV: Atelier Degas, Vente II, Paris, 11–13 December 1918, no. 154, repr.; Paris, Bernheim Jeune; London, Independent Gallery; Manchester, Whitworth Art Gallery, purchased 1926 (D. 3.1926). LIT: L. 1140, repr.; Pickvance, 1964, p. 162, repr.; Thomson, 1981¹, no. 14, repr. EXH: *Degas, Pastels and Drawings*, 1969, no. 21, repr.
Lent by the Whitworth Art Gallery, University of Manchester.

23. Landscape (Paysage). *c.*1890–3. Plate 82.
Pastel over monotype in oil colours.
Signed below: 'Degas'.

PROV: London, Percy Moore Turner. LIT: *Degas Monotypes*, 1968, no. 278 (repr.); Adhémar-Cachin, 1974, p. 283.
Private Collection.

ERNEST-ANGE DUEZ (1843–96)

Born in Paris. Pupil of Pils. Exhibited at the Salon with increasing success from 1868. Began by painting religious, historical and allegorical subjects, but later also specialised in landscapes and portraits. Participated in decorative schemes for public buildings in Paris. Executed a number of pastels and watercolours, as well as designs for manufactured goods.

24. Hydrangeas. *c.*1888. Plate 62.
Pastel. 54 × 73.5 cm. Signed lower left: 'E. Duez'.
PROV: Paris, Comtesse Greffulhe; Comte de Gramont; London, Hazlitt, Gooden and Fox, 1982. EXH: ?*Société des Pastellistes Français, Vᵉ année*, Paris, Galerie Georges Petit, 1889.
Private Collection.

IGNACE-HENRI-THÉODORE FANTIN-LATOUR (1836–1904)

Born in Grenoble. Son of a French painter of Italian descent and a Russian mother. Pupil of Lecoq de Boisbaudron, but chiefly influenced by Courbet. Intense copyist in the Musée du Louvre. Close friend of Manet and other Impressionist painters and included in the Salon des Refusés (1863), but only exhibited regularly at the official Salon. Frequently worked in England and exhibited at the Royal Academy. Painted portraits, still lifes, and fantasy subjects inspired by music, particularly Wagner. Prolific printmaker.

25. Tannhäuser on the Venusberg. 1863. Plate 26.
Black chalk and wash. 41.9 × 51.5 cm. Signed and dated in black chalk lower right: 'Fantin 1863'.
PROV: D. Croal Thompson (1924). LIT: Gibson, 1924, pp. 134–5.
RELATED WORKS: *Tannhäuser on the Venusberg*, oil, 1864 (Los Angeles, County Museum of Art; *Fantin-Latour*, 1983, no. 50); *Tannhäuser on the Venusberg* (first plate), lithograph, 1862 (*Fantin-Latour*, 1983, no. 46); *Tannhäuser on the Venusberg* (second plate), lithograph, 1876 (*Fantin-Latour*, 1983, no. 107). For other related drawings see *Fantin-Latour*, 1983, no. 49.
Lent by the City of Bristol Museum & Art Gallery.

JEAN-LOUIS FORAIN (1852–1931)

Painter, printmaker, illustrator and caricaturist. Born in Rheims and trained variously under Gérôme, Carpeaux and Gill. Close friend of Degas and included in four Impressionist exhibitions (1879, 1880, 1881, 1886). His satirical drawings of modern life appeared mainly in *Le Figaro* and *Le Courrier Français*: also published two papers of his own. Later painted several law-court scenes, but also religious subjects and themes inspired by the war of 1914–18.

26. Theatre Foyer (Couloir de théâtre). *c.*1880–1. Plate 30.
Watercolour and gouache with pencil, pen and ink. 22.2 × 35.5 cm. Signed upper right: 'L. Forain'.
PROV: Paris, Arthur Meyer; Cleveland, Ohio, King Collection; New York, Hirshl

---

and Adler; London, Hazlitt Gallery, 1973. LIT: J.-K. Huysmans, *L'Exposition des Indépendants en 1881* (Huysmans, 1929, VI, p. 270). EXH: *6ᵉ Exposition de Peinture*, Paris, 1881, no. 23
Private Collection.

27. Man in a State of Happy Repose. 1881. Plate 29.
Pastel and black chalk on buff paper.
30.5 × 46.4 cm. Signed lower left: 'forain/81'.
PROV: Amsterdam, Van Wisselingh and Co.; London, Hazlitt Gallery, 1965; Lord Goodman.
Lent by Lord Goodman.

PAUL GAUGUIN (1848–1903)

Born in Paris: his mother was of half Peruvian-Spanish descent. Spent early years at sea, 1865–71, before working in a stockbroker's office in Paris. Encouraged as a painter by Camille Pissarro during 1870s, but also influenced by Degas and Cézanne. Fully committed to painting from 1883 but contributed to five Impressionist exhibitions in all (1879, 1880, 1881, 1882, 1886). Formed important collection of paintings. Also important as printmaker and sculptor. Subsequently lived and worked at various times in Copenhagen, Brittany, Arles (with Van Gogh), Martinique and Tahiti. At Pont-Aven in Brittany during the late 1880s devised new style of painting known as *Synthétisme*.

28. Study for Four Breton Women. 1886. Plate 10.
Coloured chalk. 48 × 32 cm.
PROV: Paris, Joseph Hessel; Bernheim Jeune, by 1928; New York, Knoedler, 1929; Sir William Burrell, 1936; Glasgow, Burrell Collection (35/264). LIT: Rewald, 1958, pl. 10 (as *c.*1888); Bodelsen, 1964, pp. 26, 52, repr. fig. 10; Pickvance, 1970, p. 20, pl. II.
EXH: *Gauguin and the Pont-Aven Group*, 1966, no. 43, repr.; *Treasures from the Burrell Collection*, 1975, no. 61, repr.
RELATED WORKS: sketch in *Gauguin. Carnet*, 1962, p. 55; charcoal/pastel, 1886 (Sotheby's, 7 April 1966, no. 108, repr.); *Four Breton Women*, oil, 1886 (Munich, Bayrische Staatsgemäldesammlungen; W. 201); *Vase with Breton Women*, glazed stoneware, 1886–7 (Brussels, Musées Royaux; Bodelsen, 1964, no. 9); *Breton Women and a Calf*, oil, 1888 (Copenhagen, Ny Carlsberg Glyptotek; W. 252); *Landscape at Pont-Aven*, oil, 1888 (Berne, Koerfer Collection; W. 253); *Breton Women at a Gate*, zincograph, 1889.
Lent by The Burrell Collection, Glasgow Museums and Art Galleries.

HENRI GERVEX (1852–1929)

Born in Paris. Pupil of Brissot and Cabanel. Frequent contributor to the Salon from 1873 onwards winning many important public commissions in Paris and receiving major official honours. Painted mainly historical and mythological scenes, as well as fashionable genre subjects and portraits. His painting, *Rolla*, was refused by the Salon in 1878, owing to its risqué subject-matter (inspired by Alfred de Musset), which proved to be a *succès de scandale*. Visited Russia in 1896 and 1897. Friend of Manet, Zola and Maupassant.

29. Portrait of a Lady in a Hat. 1885. Plate 61.
Pastel on buff paper. 54.2 × 43.7 cm.

Signed and dated lower left: 'H. Gervex 1885'.
PROV: France, private collection; London, Hazlitt, Gooden and Fox, 1976.
Private Collection.

ARMAND GUILLAUMIN (1841–1927)

Only a part-time artist before 1891. Showed at Salon des Refusés, 1863, and at Impressionist exhibitions of 1874, 1877, 1880, 1881, 1882, 1886. Painted mostly landscapes in environs of Paris until 1891, then travelled in Provence, Brittany, Auvergne, Haute-Loire. Visited Holland in 1903–4. First one-man exhibition at Galerie Durand-Ruel in 1894. Died in Paris, the last surviving member of the original Impressionist group.

30. Le Quai de Bercy. 1867. Plate 47.
Pastel. 23.8 × 28.2 cm. Signed and dated lower right: 'Guillaumin/67'.
PROV: London, Redfern Gallery; Manchester, Miss Margaret Pilkington, by whom presented, 1951 (D.4.1951). LIT: Thomson, 1981[1], no. 36.
RELATED WORKS: *Barges on the Seine*, pastel, 1865, signed and dated lower right (Paris, Petit Palais; Boucher and Imbert, 1983, no. 44, repr.).
Lent by the Whitworth Art Gallery, University of Manchester.

JOHAN BARTHOLD JONGKIND (1819–91)

Born in Holland, but worked extensively in France where he died. Pupil of Shelfhout in Holland and of Eugène Isabey in France. Exhibited at the Salon from 1848. Principally a landscape painter: a prolific watercolourist.

31. Landscape near La Côte-Saint-André (Dauphiné) [Route au printemps: 'Le Murier']. 1880. Plate 66.
Watercolour and bodycolour over black chalk. Inscribed lower left: 'Le Murier'; dated lower right: '29 juin 1880' and signed 'Jongkind'.
PROV: Paris, Jean Dollfus; Paris, Galerie Hector Brame; Paris, César de Hauke, by whom bequeathed, 1968 (1968. 2.10.29). LIT: Hulton, 1968, no. 10.
RELATED WORKS: Hefting, 1975, nos. 726–7, 732–3; *L'Église de Gillonay*, 1888 (Moreau-Nélaton, 1918, fig. 151); *Un chemin en hiver avec fond montagneux*, watercolour, '3 fév. 1880' (Paris, Petit Palais).
Lent by the Trustees of the British Museum, London.

CHARLES-ALBERT LEBOURG (1849–1928)

Born in Normandy. Trained to be an architect, but encouraged to become a landscape painter. Taught drawing at the Société des Beaux-Arts in Algiers, 1872–7. Received further instruction, mainly in drawing, upon his return to France from Laurens. Exhibited with the Impressionists in 1879 and 1880. Later many works accepted by the Salon. Mostly painted motifs along the banks of the Seine. Worked in Holland, 1895–7, and visited England, 1900. Paralysed during last years of his life.

32. The Artist's Wife and Mother-in-Law Reading a Letter by Candlelight. c.1879. Plate 60.

Black chalk heightened with white on buff paper. 43.5 × 28.3 cm. Signed lower left: 'a. lebourg'.
PROV: Paris, Étienne Moreau-Nélaton; London, Hazlitt, Gooden and Fox, 1978; London, British Museum. (1978-10-7-3).
LIT: Bénédite, 1923, no. 2085; Thomson, 1985, p. 30, repr. p. 31. EXH: *4e Exposition de la Peinture*, Paris, 1879, no. 130?
RELATED WORKS: Bénédite, 1923, no. 2063.
Lent by the Trustees of the British Museum, London.

LÉON LHERMITTE (1844–1925)

Pupil of Lecoq de Boisbaudran. Exhibited *fusains* (charcoal drawings) at the Salon, 1866–89, as well as paintings. Visited London several times from 1869 and achieved great popularity in Britain. In contact with Degas c.1879–83 and may have been invited to exhibit at 1879 Impressionist exhibition. Painted mainly peasant subjects that influenced Van Gogh among others. Much honoured in France for his large-scale decorative paintings, and widely acclaimed throughout Europe.

33. Interior: Nine Peasant Women Seated in a Church. 1867. Plate 38.
Black chalk. 26 × 46.3 cm. Signed and dated lower left: 'L.Lhermitte. 67' (by another hand?).
PROV: M. Trélat, by whom presented 1868.
LIT: Hamel, 1974, p. 19 no. 2: ten-Doesschate Chu, 1982, fig. 9.12. EXH: *Peasant in French 19th Century Art*, 1980, no. 49.
RELATED WORKS: two studies in a private collection, Paris (see *Peasant in French 19th Century Art*, 1980, under no. 49); *Peasant Women Seated in a Church*, black chalk, c.1867 (exh. New York, Shepherd Gallery, *19th Century French and other Continental Drawings, Watercolours and Oil Sketches*, 1979, no. 85, repr).
Lent by the Victoria and Albert Museum, London.

ÉDOUARD MANET (1832–83)

Born in Paris, son of a government official. Pupil of Couture. Profoundly influenced by Old Masters. Exhibited at Salon des Refusés, 1863, and held a private exhibition at the Paris World's Fair of 1867. Continued to submit his paintings to the Salon, even though they were sometimes rejected. His style became more closely allied to Impressionism during the mid-1870s, but he did not participate in any of the Impressionist exhibitions. Painter primarily of portraits, scenes from contemporary life and still-lifes. Also executed a number of pastels and prints. Died after a long illness.

34. Study of a Woman at her Toilet. 1862. Plate 32.
Red chalk (incised outlines). 29 × 20.8 cm.
PROV: Paris, Marcel Guiot; London, Leicester Galleries; London, Samuel Courtauld, 1928, by whom bequeathed, 1948. EXH: *Manet, Das graphischen Werk*, 1977, no. Z.7; *Manet*, 1978, no. 4; *Mantegna to Cézanne*, 1983, no. 109; *The Impressionists and the Post-Impressionists from The Courtauld Institute*, 1984, no. 51.
LIT: Guérin, 1944, under no. 26; Cooper, 1954, no. 140, pp. 142–3; de Leiris, 1969, pp. 19, 31, 41, 57, 58, 59, 63 and no. 185;

Harris, 1970, under no. 20; R/W II, no. 360; *Manet 1832–1883*, 1983, under no. 25.
RELATED WORKS: *La Toilette*, etching (Harris, 1970, no. 20). Possibly related, R/W II, nos. 358–9, 361–3, although certain of these drawings might have been made in connection with *La Nymphe surprise*, oil, 1861 (Buenos Aires, Museo de Bellas Artes; R/W I, no. 40) or with a projected composition of *The Finding of Moses*.
Lent by the Courtauld Institute Galleries (Samuel Courtauld Collection).

35. Don Mariano Camprubi. 1862. Plate 31.
Brush drawing in dark ink with some highlights in gouache. 16.5 × 15.2 cm. Stamp lower left: 'E.M.' (Lugt 880).
PROV: Paris, Édouard Manet (Paris, 4–5 February 1884, no. 144); Paris, Jacques Doucet (Paris, 28–29 December 1917, no. 239); Paris, Bernstein, 1917; Paris, Paul Rosenberg; Glasgow, Sir William Burrell, acquired 1923; Glasgow, Burrell Collection (35/313). LIT: Guérin, 1944, under no. 24; Tabarant, 1947, p. 54 and no. 560; de Leiris, 1969, p. 58 and no. 180, p. 107; Harris, 1970, under no. 34; R/W II, no. 461; *Manet 1832–1883*, 1983, under no. 49.
RELATED WORKS: *Portrait of Don Mariano Camprubi*, oil, 1862 (Mr and Mrs Donald Stralem, New York; R/W I, no. 54); *Le Ballet espagnol*, oil, 1862 (Washington, Phillips Collection; R/W I, no. 55); *Don Mariano Camprubi*, etching (Harris, 1970, no. 34).
Lent by The Burrell Collection, Glasgow Museums and Art Galleries.

36. Le Déjeuner sur l'herbe. 1863. Plate 2.
Pen and ink and watercolour over indications in black chalk. 40.8 × 48 cm.
PROV: Paris, Portier, c.1900; Eugène Blot (Paris, 10 May 1906, no. 105, bt. Bernardt); Berlin, Bruno Cassirer; Oxford, Dr and Mrs R. Walzer. Accepted by H.M. Government in lieu of Capital Transfer Tax from the estate of Dr and Mrs R. Walzer and presented to the Ashmolean Museum, Oxford, 1980. LIT: Tabarant, 1947, pp. 72, 513, 549 and no. 568; de Leiris, 1969, no. 197; R/W II, no. 306. EXH: *Manet*, 1978, no. 9; *Manet 1832–1882*, 1983, no. 63.
RELATED WORKS: *Le Déjeuner sur l'herbe*, oil, 1863 (London, Courtauld Institute Galleries; R/W I, no. 66); *Le Déjeuner sur l'herbe*, oil, 1863 (Paris, Musée d'Orsay; R/W I, no. 67).
Lent by the Visitors of The Ashmolean Museum, Oxford.

37. A Café, Place du Théâtre-Français. c.1877–8. Plate 43.
Pastel on canvas. 32.4 × 45.7 cm. Signed lower right: 'Manet'.
PROV: Paris, Ambroise Vollard; London, Arthur Kay; Paris, Paul Rosenberg; Bernheim Jeune; Sir William Burrell; Glasgow, Burrell Collection (35/306). LIT: Tabarant, 1947, p. 431, no. 519; R/W II, no. 64 (as 1880–1); *Manet, 1832–1883*, 1983, pp. 409–10 (as c.1877–8). EXH: *Treasures from the Burrell Collection*, 1975, no. 49, repr.
RELATED WORKS: pencil and wash *croquis*, c.1877–8 (Paris, Louvre, Cabinet des Dessins; R/W II, no. 528).
Lent by The Burrell Collection, Glasgow Museums and Art Galleries.

38. A Man on Crutches. 1878. Plate 45.
Pen and ink with light pencil
underdrawing. 27 × 19.2 cm. Signed
lower right: 'Ed. Manet'. Inscribed
lower left: 'au moment/ de la fête'.
PROV: sold Christie's, 26 April 1935, no. 47;
Oxford, Ashmolean Museum, purchased
1935. LIT: Parker, I, 1938, no. 596; Mathey,
1963, no. 71, repr.
RELATED WORKS: *The Rue Mosnier Decked
out with Flags*, oil, 1878 (Upperville,
Virginia, Mellon Collection; R/W I, no.
270); brush and ink drawing, 1878 (New
York, Metropolitan Museum; R/W II, no.
479); pencil, brush and ink drawing, 1878
(Paris, private collection; R/W II, no. 478).
Lent by the Visitors of The Ashmolean
Museum, Oxford.

**39. Two Women drinking Beer (Les
Bockeuses).** 1878. Plate 17.
Pastel on canvas. 61 × 50.8 cm. Signed
lower right: 'Manet'.
PROV: sold by Manet to a Dutch collector,
1880; Paris, Paul Rosenberg; Ambroise
Vollard; London, Arthur Kay, by 1901; Sir
William Burrell; Glasgow, Burrell
Collection (35/305). LIT: Tabarant, 1947, p.
330, no. 465; R/W II, no. 7; Gronberg, 1984,
p. 335. EXH: *Oeuvres nouvelles d'Édouard
Manet*, Paris, La Vie Moderne, 1880, no. 23;
Treasures from the Burrell Collection, 1975,
no. 48, repr.
Lent by The Burrell Collection, Glasgow
Museums and Art Galleries.

40. Mlle Suzette Lemaire, full face.
*c.*1880. Plate 76.
Pastel on canvas. 53 × 33 cm. Signed
lower right: 'Manet'.
PROV: Paris, Charles Ephrussi; Paul
Gallimard; Paul Rosenberg; Berlin, Bruno
Cassirer; Great Britain, private collection.
LIT: Blanche, 1919, pp. 137–8; Tabarant,
1947, p. 429, no. 512; R/W II, no. 43. EXH:
Manet at Work, 1983, no. 25, repr.
Private Collection.

41. Marie Colombier. 1880. Plate 40.
Pastel on canvas. 53 × 34 cm. Signed
lower left: 'Manet'.
PROV: Paris, Marie Colombier; Auguste
Pellerin; Bernheim Jeune, by 1910; Sir
William Burrell; Glasgow, Burrell
Collection (35/309). LIT: Tabarant, 1947, p.
397, no. 489; R/W II, no. 38. EXH: *Oeuvres
nouvelles d'Édouard Manet*, Paris, La Vie
Moderne, 1880, no. 25; *Exposition post-
hume Manet*, Paris, École des Beaux-Arts,
1884, no. 139; *Treasures from the Burrell
Collection*, 1975, no. 51, repr.
RELATED WORKS: pen and ink studies,
*c.*1880 (Oxford, Ashmolean Museum; R/W
II, no. 420; Paris, private collection; R/W
II, no. 421; location unknown; R/W II, no.
422).
Lent by The Burrell Collection, Glasgow
Museums and Art Galleries.

CLAUDE-OSCAR MONET (1840–1926)
Born in Paris, but first influenced by
Boudin and Jongkind at Le Havre. Pupil for
a time of Charles Gleyre. Lived for long
periods at Argenteuil, Vétheuil and
Giverny. Exhibited at five of the
Impressionist exhibitions (missed 1880,
1881, 1886). Also worked in England,
Holland, Italy and Norway. Gained con-
siderable financial success by *c.*1890 when
he also began to paint pictures in series.
Principally a landscape artist.

42. Sunset over the Sea. 1865–70.
Plate 14.
Pastel and gouache on buff-coloured
paper. 17.2 × 33.2 cm. Signed lower
right: 'C. Monet'.
PROV: Seaford (Sussex), F. Hindley Smith,
by whom bequeathed, 1939. EXH:
Impressionism, 1974, no. 67; *Dürer to
Cézanne*, 1983, no. 112.
RELATED WORK: possibly, *Marine*, oil,
*c.*1865 (Copenhagen, Ordrupgaard-
samlingen; W. 72).
Lent by the Visitors of The Ashmolean
Museum, Oxford.

BERTHE MORISOT (1841–95)
Born in Bourges. Pupil of Corot from 1861,
but later became acquainted with Manet,
whose younger brother, Eugène, she mar-
ried in 1874. Later influenced by Renoir.
Painted mainly landscapes and domestic
genre scenes exhibiting work at seven of
the Impressionist exhibitions (missed
1879). Close friend of Mallarmé. Died in
Paris.

43. Carriage in the Bois de Boulogne.
*c.*1874 or later. Plate 5.
Watercolour. 28.9 × 20.7 cm. Inscribed
on verso: 'Bois de Boulogne/BM'.
Stamp lower left: 'B.M.' (Lugt 388a).
PROV: Oxford, Mrs H. H. Turner, by whom
bequeathed, 1959. EXH: *Première
Exposition*, 1874, nos. 111–12(?).
RELATED WORKS: *L'Allée des Poteaux, au
Bois de Boulogne*, oil, 1889 (B/W 780);
Promeneuse, watercolour (Paris, private
collection; P. Huisman, *Morisot, Charmes*,
Lausanne, 1972, p. 36, repr.).
Lent by the Visitors of The Ashmolean
Museum, Oxford.

44. Isabelle. 1885. Plate 67.
Pastel. 40 × 29.8 cm. Signed lower
right: 'Berthe Morisot'.
PROV: Paris, Jacques-Émile Blanche;
London, Hugh Walpole; Lord and Lady
Sainsbury; University of East Anglia,
Robert and Lisa Sainsbury Collection. EXH:
Berthe Morisot, Paris, Durand-Ruel, 1902,
no. 64. LIT: B/W 946, pl. 463.
Lent by the Robert and Lisa Sainsbury
Collection, University of East Anglia.

**45. Study of Two Girls Writing at a
Table.** *c.*1890. Plate 69.
Pencil heightened with pastel.
20.7 × 26.5 cm. Verso: *Head of the
Artist's Daughter, Julie*. Pencil
heightened with pastel.
RELATED WORK: *Young Girl Seated at a Table*,
pencil on buff paper, 29.2 × 40.6 cm.,
*c.*1890 (Chicago, The Art Institute, inv.
1963.921).
Private Collection.

CAMILLE PISSARRO (1830–1903)
Born on the island of St Thomas (Virgin
Islands). Pupil of Fritz Melbye. Settled in
France, 1855. Encouraged by Corot.
Showed at Salon des Refusés, 1863, and at
all Impressionist exhibitions, 1874–86.
Subsequently exhibited with the *Les Vingt*
group in Brussels. Mainly landscape painter until *c.*1880, when figure subjects took
on major significance. Neo-Impressionist
phase, *c.*1886–90.

**46. Study of a Male Nude Posed
against a Wall Seen in Profile Facing
Right.** 1855–60. Plate 18.
Charcoal heightened in places with
white on blue paper. 46.8 × 29.5 cm.

Stamp lower right: 'CP' (Lugt 613a).
PROV: London, Lucien Pissarro and thence
by descent to his widow, Esther, by whom
presented, 1950. LIT: B/L 37. EXH:
Retrospective Camille Pissarro, 1984, no. 72.
RELATED WORKS: B/L 36 and 38 (with re-
ferences to further drawings).
Lent by the Visitors of The Ashmolean
Museum, Oxford.

47. Chailly. *c.*1857. Plate 22.
Charcoal on beige paper. 31.5 × 48.8
cm. Inscribed and signed lower left:
'Chailly C. Pissarro'. Verso: *Brief Study
of a Horse Seen in Three-quarters Profile
Facing Right*. Pencil.
PROV: London, Lucien Pissarro and thence
by descent to his widow, Esther, by whom
presented, 1950. LIT: B/L 60. EXH: *Camille
Pissarro, 1830–1903*, 1980–1, no. 102.
RELATED WORKS: possibly *Paysage aux en-
virons de Paris*, oil, 1857 (P & V 11); *Study of
a Tree c.1857*, charcoal (Upperville,
Virginia, Mellon Collection); *Study of a
Group of Trees, c.*1857, charcoal on grey
paper (Upperville, Virginia, Mellon
Collection); *Study of Trees at Chailly*,
*c.*1857, charcoal on beige paper, inscribed
'Chailly' lower left (Sotheby Parke-Bernet,
12 May 1977, no. 211).
Lent by the Visitors of The Ashmolean
Museum, Oxford.

48. Nanterre. *c.*1860. Plate 21.
Charcoal heightened with white chalk
on grey paper. 24.3 × 30.9 cm.
Inscribed lower right: 'Nanterre'.
Stamp lower right: 'CP' (Lugt 613e).
PROV: London, Lucien Pissarro and thence
by descent to his widow, Esther, by whom
presented, 1950. LIT: B/L 61. EXH: *Camille
Pissarro, 1830–1903*, 1980–1, no. 103;
Retrospective Camille Pissarro, 1984, no. 74.
Lent by the Visitors of The Ashmolean
Museum, Oxford.

49. Apple-picking. 1870–5. Plate 57.
Pastel with black and white chalk on
buff-coloured paper. 34.2 × 49.4 cm.
Stamp lower right: 'CP' (Lugt 613a).
PROV: Paris, Ludovic-Rodolphe Pissarro;
London, Wildenstein; London, Desmond
Coke; London, Redfern Gallery; York, City
Art Gallery, purchased 1950 (inv. R. 2027).
EXH: *Camille Pissarro, 1830–1903*, 1980–1,
no. 106.
Lent by York City Art Gallery.

50. Portrait of Mlle Marie Daudon.
1876. Plate 15.
Pastel. 36.8 × 25.3 cm. Signed and dated
lower left: 'C. Pissarro/1er Janvier 1876'.
PROV: London, Lucien Pissarro and thence
by descent to his widow, Esther, by whom
presented, 1950. LIT: P & V 1534; B/L 72.
RELATED WORKS: *Portrait of Mlle Marie
Daudon Seated on a Chair*, pencil, *c.*1865,
signed and inscribed lower right: 'C.
Pissarro/Marie Daudon' (London, J. P. L.
Fine Arts, *A Selection of Drawings,
Watercolours and Pastels by Camille
Pissarro c.1853–1903*, 1978, no. 2).
Lent by the Visitors of The Ashmolean
Museum, Oxford.

**51. Le Boulevard de Clichy, effet de
soleil d'hiver.** 1880. Plate 6.
Pastel. 60 × 75 cm. Signed and dated
lower left: 'C. Pissarro.80'.
PROV: Paris, Marc François (Paris, 20 March
1935, no. 10); London, Reid and Lefevre.
LIT: P & V 1545. EXH: *6^e Exposition de*

Peinture, Paris, 1881, no. 90 (entitled 'Boulevard Rochechouart').
RELATED WORKS: *Study of Le Boulevard de Clichy*, no details known (formerly Lucien Pissarro Collection (Courtauld neg. no. 52/45(3a)).
Private Collection.

52. Sheet of Studies including Figures Harvesting. 1882. Plate 78.
Black chalk and charcoal with some watercolour. 31.3 × 21 cm. Stamp lower right: 'CP' (Lugt 613a).
PROV: London, Lucien Pissarro and thence by descent to his widow, Esther, by whom presented, 1950. LIT: B/L 115.
RELATED WORK: *La Moisson*, tempera, 1882 (Tokyo, National Museum of Western Art; P & V 1358).
Lent by the Visitors of The Ashmolean Museum, Oxford.

53. Study for 'The Harvest'. *c.*1882. Plate 55.
Black chalk on pink paper with a thin layer of chinese white. 42.8 × 63.8 cm. Signed lower left: 'C.P.'
PROV: London, Lucien Pissarro and thence by descent to his widow, Esther, by whom presented, 1950. LIT: B/L 123; Lloyd, 1981, p. 94, repr. EXH: *Camille Pissarro, 1830–1903*, 1980–1, no. 120, repr.; *Retrospective Camille Pissarro*, 1984, no. 81, repr.
RELATED WORKS: black chalk and wash drawings, B/L 122 and *Camille Pissarro. Drawings, Watercolours and Pastels* (J. P. L. Fine Arts, London, 1984), p. 21 above and below; pastel, *c.*1882 (location unknown; P & V 1558); *The Harvest*, tempera, 1882 (Tokyo, National Museum of Western Art; P & V 1358); *The Mower*, lithograph, *c.*1894 (Delteil, 1923, no. 141); gouache, *c.*1894 (P & V 1474).
Lent by the Visitors of The Ashmolean Museum, Oxford.

54. Spring: Peasant Women in a Field. 1882. Plate 79.
Black chalk, gouache and tempera on silk. 24.2 × 53.3 cm. (fan-shaped). Signed and dated lower left: 'C. Pissarro, 1882'.
PROV: London, Lucien Pissarro; Oxford, Sir Basil Blackwell; London, J. P. L. Fine Arts, 1980.
Lent by Mr and Mrs Julian Sofaer.

55. The Market Stall. 1884. Plate 1.
Tempera and watercolour over black chalk on board. 61 × 48.2 cm. Signed and dated lower left: 'C. Pissarro/1884'.
PROV: France, Pissarro family; Sir William Burrell, by whom presented to Glasgow Corporation, 1925; Glasgow, Burrell Collection (35/592). LIT: undated (1884) letter from Gauguin to Pissarro (*Archives de Camille Pissarro*, 1975, no. 53; letter from Pissarro to Durand-Ruel, early June 1885 (*Pissarro Correspondance*, 1980, p. 335); P & V 1389.
RELATED WORK: black chalk drawing, *c.*1884 (*Pissarro in England*, 1968, no. 44, repr.).
Lent by The Burrell Collection, Glasgow Museums and Art Galleries.

56. Four Seated Peasant Women. *c.*1885.
Pastel and gouache. 47.5 × 47.5 cm. Signed upper left: 'C. Pissarro'.
PROV: London, Lucien Pissarro; Orovida Pissarro. LIT: P & V 1571.

RELATED WORK: *Peasant Women Resting*, tempera, *c.*1885 (P & V 1399).
Private Collection.

57. The Corn Stooks (Les Moyettes). *c.*1887. Plate 48.
Pastel on silk. 23.6 × 29.5 cm. Signed lower left: 'C. Pissarro'.
PROV: London, Lucien Pissarro; Manchester, Miss Margaret Pilkington by whom presented to the Whitworth Art Gallery, Manchester (D. 9.1943). LIT: P & V 1605; Thomson, 1980, p. 260, pl. 43; Thomson, 1981¹, no. 57, repr.
RELATED WORKS: black chalk drawing (formerly Lucien Pissarro; Courtauld neg. no. 52/43(33)); *Harvest at Eragny*, fan, 1887 (P & V 1639); watercolours no. 58 below and *Pissarro in England*, 1968, no. 37, repr.; *The Gleaners*, oil, 1889 (Basle, Kunstmuseum; P & V 730).
Lent by the Whitworth Art Gallery, University of Manchester.

58. Landscape with Ploughed Field, Eragny. *c.*1887–8. Plate 46.
Watercolour over pencil. 20.9 × 47.6 cm. Numbered and signed lower right: 'No. 14. C. Pissarro'.
PROV: Oxford, Ashmolean Museum, purchased 1945. LIT: B/L 191. EXH: *Camille Pissarro, 1830–1903*, 1980–1, no. 134, repr.
RELATED WORK: see no. 57 above.
Lent by the Visitors of The Ashmolean Museum, Oxford.

59. Peasant Women Planting Pea Sticks in the Ground. 1890. Plate 11.
Gouache and black chalk on grey-brown paper. 39 × 60.2 cm. (fan-shaped). Signed and dated lower right: 'C. Pissarro. 1890'.
PROV: London, Lucien Pissarro and thence by descent to his widow, Esther, by whom presented, 1950. LIT: letter from Lucien to Camille Pissarro, January 1891 (Pissarro, 1950, pp. 201–3); B/L 219. EXH: *Camille Pissarro, 1830–1903*, 1980–1, no. 212, repr.
RELATED WORK: *Peasant Women Planting Pea Sticks*, oil, 1891 (P & V 772).
Lent by the Visitors of The Ashmolean Museum, Oxford.

60. Study for 'Peasant Women Chatting in a Farmyard, Eragny'. *c.*1895. Plate 72.
Black chalk and pastel on pink paper. 45.7 × 43.8 cm.
PROV: London, Leicester Galleries, by 1920; Gregynog Hall, Montgomeryshire, Gwendoline and Margaret Davies by whom bequeathed, 1963. LIT: Ingamells, 1967, p. 72, pl. 24a. EXH: *Retrospective Camille Pissarro*, 1984, no. 99, repr.
RELATED WORKS: *Peasant Women in a Farmyard*, gouache, 1888 (New York, Metropolitan Museum, inv. 1980.21.15); *Peasant Women Chatting in a Farmyard, Eragny*, oil, 1895/1902 (P & V 1272).
Lent by the National Museum of Wales, Cardiff.

LUCIEN PISSARRO (1863–1944)

Eldest son of Camille Pissarro. Included at the final Impressionist exhibition, 1886. Trained by his father, but also influenced by Seurat. Painted in the Neo-Impressionist style, 1885–91, and was involved with the *Les Vingt* group in Brussels. Spent time in England, intermittently from 1883, but settled in London permanently in 1890. Prolific book-illustrator and founder of the

Eragny Press. Exerted a considerable influence on English painting, especially the Fitzroy Street Group and the Camden Town Group.

61a. Il était une bergère. (There Once Was a Shepherdess). *c.*1886.
Plates 49a–d.
Title page: pen, ink and watercolour. 22 × 18.7 cm. Inscribed: 'Il était une/Bergère/Illustrations/de Lucien Pissarro'.
61b. She Went to Make a Cheese: pen, ink and watercolour. 20.5 × 17.1 cm. Inscribed lower right: 'L.P.'
61c. The Shepherdess Lost her Temper: pen, ink and watercolour. 21 × 17.3 cm.
61d. We'll Embrace in Forgiveness: pen, ink and watercolour. 20.4 × 16.9 cm.
PROV: London, Lucien Pissarro and thence by descent to his widow, Esther, by whom presented, Oxford, 1950. LIT: Ajalbert, 1886, p. 391; Chambers, 1980, pp. 18–19. EXH: 8ᵉ *Exposition de la Peinture*, Paris, 1886, no. 116 (as *Projet d'illustration*).
RELATED WORKS: numerous studies in the Ashmolean Museum and private collection, Oxford; partial wood engraving of cover illustration (repr. Chambers, 1980, p. 19).
Lent by the Visitors of The Ashmolean Museum, Oxford.

PIERRE PUVIS DE CHAVANNES (1824–98)

Born in Lyons. Studied briefly with H. Scheffer and Couture, but was more profoundly influenced by Chassériau. Exhibited at the Salon, but did not achieve success until the 1860s. Famed for his large-scale mural decorations executed for public buildings both in France (Amiens, Marseilles, Lyons, Rouen, Paris) and America (Boston). Cultivating the style of a fresco painter, his allegorical compositions inspired many younger painters, among them Seurat, Gauguin, Denis and Picasso.

62. Solitude. *c.*1879–83. Plate 73.
Pastel on buff paper laid down on canvas, lightly squared. 32 × 41.3 cm. Signed lower right: 'P. Puvis de Chavannes'.
PROV: Vente, Paris, 16–17 December 1919, no. 198, repr.; London, Independent Gallery; Manchester, Whitworth Art Gallery, purchased 1921 (D. 22.1921). LIT: Boucher, 1979, p. 68; Thomson, 1981¹, no. 65.
RELATED WORKS: drawings in Paris, Louvre, Cabinet des Dessins (inv. RF. 2324), Petit Palais (Boucher, 1979, no. 80, repr.) and France, private collection (*Puvis de Chavannes, 1824–1898*, 1977, no. 130, repr.); *The Prodigal Son*, oil, *c.*1879–83 (Washington, National Gallery of Art).
Lent by the Whitworth Art Gallery, University of Manchester.

63. Study for 'The Sacred Grove' (Le Bois sacré). *c.*1882–4. Plate 71.
Charcoal on brown paper laid down on canvas (pigment splashes to lower left). 57 × 117.5 cm. Signed and inscribed lower left: 'Première pensée du bois sacré/P. Puvis de Chavannes'.
PROV: London, Lady Kathleen Epstein/ Sally Ryan, by whom bequeathed, 1973 (GR. 192). LIT: Vigurs, 1976, p. 97.
RELATED WORKS: *Le Bois sacré cher aux Arts*

et aux Muses, oil, 1884 (Lyons, Musée des Beaux-Arts). For other studies see Boucher, 1979, p. 88. A black chalk drawing in Rotterdam, Boymans-van Beuningen Museum (F. II.85; Hoetink, 1968, no. 218, repr.), is directly related to no. 63.
Lent by the Garman-Ryan Collection, Walsall Museum and Art Gallery.

JEAN-FRANÇOIS RAFFAËLLI (1850–1924)

Born and died in Paris. Pupil of Gérôme. Works frequently accepted by the Salon during the 1870s. Also inspired by the Impressionists, especially Degas, and exhibited in the 1880 and 1881 exhibitions. At first painted historical genre scenes and then more realistic subjects observed in the industrial suburbs of Paris, but after a successful one-man exhibition in 1884 concentrated on more fashionable motifs, especially views of Paris. An artist of multifarious interests, including illustration, printmaking and sculpture, he held advanced views on the role of art in society and was friendly with Naturalist writers. Twice visited America, 1895 and 1899.

64. Study for 'Les Types de Paris: Les Petites Marchandes des rues'. 1889. Plate 51.
Black chalk, watercolour, pen, ink and wash on buff paper. 24.5 × 23 cm. Signed lower right: 'J.F.Raffaëlli'.
PROV: London, Robert Noortman Gallery.
LIT: *Les Types de Paris*, no. 1, Paris, 1889, repr. p. 7. (The accompanying prose piece was by Henri Greville).
Private Collection.

PIERRE-AUGUSTE RENOIR (1841–1919)

Born in Limoges. Apprenticed at first to a porcelain manufacturer. Pupil of Charles Gleyre. Influenced by Delacroix and Courbet. Exhibited at four of the Impressionist exhibitions (1874, 1876, 1877, 1882), but was also highly successful at the Salon. Later exhibited with *Les Vingt* in Brussels. Landscape and portrait painter, but also depicted contemporary scenes. During early 1880s preoccupied with more formal compositions and greater precision of drawing, being influenced by Raphael, Boucher and Ingres. Visited Algeria, Italy and Spain. Undertook some sculpture. Spent considerable time during later years in the south of France where he died at Cagnes after being severely crippled with arthritis.

65. Head of a Young Woman with Red Hair. *c.*1876–8. Plate 68.
Pastel. 50.8 × 40 cm. Signed on right: 'Renoir' (partly obscured).
PROV: Glasgow, Sir William Burrell, 1927; Glasgow, Burrell Collection (35.601). LIT: Rewald, 1946, no. 5; *Glasgow Art Gallery. Catalogue of French Paintings*, 1953, p. 44. EXH: (?)Paris, *Cinquième exposition de la vie moderne, P. -A. Renoir*, 1879.
Lent by The Burrell Collection, Glasgow Museums and Art Galleries.

66. Head of a Young Woman. *c.*1878–80. Plate 41.
Pastel on white board. 57 × 47 cm. Signed lower right: 'Renoir'.
PROV: Miss Anne Thomson, by descent through the family.
Anonymous loan to the Fitzwilliam Museum, Cambridge.

67. Study of Two Circus Girls (Francisca and Angelina Wartenberg) of the Cirque Fernando. 1879. Plate 54.
Black chalk on linen-faced paper. 31.8 × 22.5 cm.
PROV: London, Kenneth Clark.
RELATED WORK: *Two Little Circus Girls*, oil, 1879 (Chicago, the Art Institute; Daulte, 1971, no. 297).
Lent from Saltwood Castle.

68. Nude Woman Seen from the back in Three-Quarters Profile Sitting Drying her Foot. 1885–90. Plate 13.
Red chalk heightened with white. 38.5 × 30.2 cm. Signed lower left: 'Renoir'
PROV: De Heeckeren; Paris, Galerie Hector Brame; Paris, César de Hauke, by whom bequeathed, 1968 (1968. 2.10.23). LIT: Rewald, 1946, no. 55; Hulton, 1968, no. 11.
RELATED WORK: another version formerly in the collection of Pierre Baudin (Paris, 16 March 1921, no. 44).
Lent by the Trustees of the British Museum, London.

69. Young Woman by a Lake. *c.*1885. Plate 74.
Watercolour. 14.1 × 18.8 cm. Signed lower right: 'Renoir'.
PROV: London, Montague Shearman, by whom bequeathed through the Contemporary Art Society, 1940. EXH: London, Redfern Gallery, *The Montague Shearman Collection of French and English Paintings*, 1940, no. 37.
RELATED WORKS: *Études: Aline Charigot, fille dans l'herbe et têtes*, oil, *c.*1881–3 (Sotheby's, 4 December, 1984, lot 7); Budapest, Museum of Fine Arts, watercolour, *c.*1886 (inv. 1935. 2762); Birmingham, City Museum and Art Gallery, watercolour, *c.*1885 (inv. P 17' 57); Rewald, 1946, pl. 51; Oberlin College, Ohio, Allen Memorial Art Museum, watercolour over pencil, *c.*1885 (62.63; Stechow, 1976, no. 279).
Lent by the Visitors of The Ashmolean Museum, Oxford.

70. The Two Sisters (formerly **The Lerolle Sisters**). *c.*1889. Plate 9.
Pastel on grey paper. 79 × 63.5 cm. Signed lower right: 'Renoir'.
PROV: London, Lady Baillie; City of Bristol Museum & Art Gallery (K. 4349).
RELATED WORK: *The Two Sisters*, oil, *c.*1889 (U.S.A., private collection; Daulte, 1971, no. 562, repr.). Neither this nor no. 70 represents the Lerolle girls, born in 1877 and 1879.
Lent by the City of Bristol Museum & Art Gallery.

71. Study for 'The Promenade'. *c.*1890. Plate 77.
Sanguine and black chalk. 44.5 × 29.75 cm. Initial lower right: 'R'.
RELATED WORKS: *The Promenade*, oil, 1890 (London, private collection; Daulte, 1971, no. 627, repr.). For drawings see Vollard, 1918, II, p. 116, repr.; Vollard, 1919, pp. 66, 243, repr.; Rotterdam, Boymans-van Beuningen Museum (F. II.23; Hoetink, 1968, no. 224, repr.).
Private Collection.

72. The Snack (La Collation). *c.*1895. Plate 37.
Sanguine and black chalk.

42.3 × 31.5 cm. Signed lower right: 'Renoir'.
PROV: London, Arnold John Hugh Smith, by whom bequeathed through the National Art-Collections Fund, 1964 (PD. 21-1964). EXH: *Cent Dessins Français*, 1976, no. 88, repr.; *European Drawings from the Fitzwilliam*, 1976–7, no. 1, repr. pl. 11.
RELATED WORKS: drawings repr. Vollard, 1918, I, no. 558; Vollard, 1919, p. 202.
Lent by the Syndics of the Fitzwilliam Museum, Cambridge.

GEORGES SEURAT (1859–91)

Born in Paris. Studied at the École des Beaux-Arts, 1878–80, as a pupil of Lehmann. Military service, 1879–80. Concentrated during early 1880s on drawing, but developed an interest in the scientific investigation of colour on the basis of which he evolved 'divisionist' and 'pointillist' styles of painting known as Neo-Impressionism. Exhibited *Dimanche à la Grande-Jatte* at last Impressionist exhibition, 1886, and included works with the *Les Vingt* group in Brussels. Founder member of Société des Artistes Indépendants, 1884, where *Une Baignade, Asnières* was exhibited. Painted scenes of contemporary life, but also marines executed on the Normandy coast.

73. Study of a Standing Female Nude Facing Left. *c.*1879. Plate 39.
Conté crayon. 63.2 × 48.2 cm. (irregular). Inscribed on verso: 'de Georges Seurat/felF' [Félix Fénéon] and numbered '381'.
PROV: London, Samuel Courtauld, by whom bequeathed, 1948. LIT: Kahn, 1928, pl. 61; Herbert, 1962, pp. 24–5, no. 23, p. 177; Thomson, 1985, pp. 27–8 repr. EXH: *Mantegna to Cézanne*, 1983, no. 111; *The Impressionists and the Post-Impressionists from The Courtauld Collection*, 1984, no. 86.
RELATED WORKS: *Outline Study of Standing Female Nude Facing Left*, pencil, *c.*1879 (Herbert, 1965, p. 25 and p. 176, no. 22).
Lent by the Courtauld Institute Galleries (Samuel Courtauld Collection).

74. The Gleaner. *c.*1882. Plate 81.
Conté crayon. 32 × 24 cm.
PROV: Paris, Paul Signac; Jacques Rodrigues-Henriquès; London, Campbell Dodgson, by whom bequeathed (1949-4-11-83). LIT: DH 559; Herbert, 1962, no. 153; Thomson, 1985, p. 28, repr. p. 29.
Lent by the Trustees of the British Museum, London.

75. Study for 'La Grande-Jatte: Landscape with Dog'. *c.*1884–5. Plate 58.
Conté crayon. 40 × 60.2 cm. Signed lower right: 'Seurat'.
PROV: Paris, Mme Seurat; Émile Seurat; Louis Bouglé; André Berthellémy; César de Hauke, by whom bequeathed, 1968 (1968. 2.10.17). LIT: D/R 116c; DH 641; Hulton, 1968, no. 12, repr.; Thomson, 1985, p. 99, 123, pl. 105. EXH: *Seurat Retrospective*, Paris, Salon des Indépendants, 1892, no. 1119; *Master Drawings and Watercolours*, 1984, no. 146, repr.
RELATED WORKS: Study for *La Grande-Jatte: Landscape*, oil, 1884 (New York, Whitney Collection; DH 131); *Sunday on the Grande-Jatte (1884)*, oil, 1884–6 (Art Institute of Chicago; DH 162).
Lent by the Trustees of the British Museum, London.

91

76. Study for 'La Grande-Jatte: The Couple'. *c.*1884–5. Plate 59.
Conté crayon. 31.1 × 23.8 cm.
PROV: Paris, Hodebert; Vente, Paris, Hôtel Drouot, 31 May 1927, no. 424; César de Hauke, by whom bequeathed, 1968 (1968. 2.10.16). LIT: D/R 135a; DH 644; Hulton, 1968, no. 13, repr.; Thomson, 1985, p. 106, fig. 116. EXH: *Drawing. Technique and Purpose*, 1981, no. 132.
RELATED WORKS: preceding explorations of this motif include drawings DH 623, 625 and oil sketches DH 135–7. The measurements on the margins of no. 76 correspond to the squaring of *Study for La Grande-Jatte: The Couple and Three Women*, oil, *c.*1884–5 (Cambridge, Fitzwilliam Museum, the Keynes Collection; DH 138). See also no. 75 above.
Lent by the Trustees of the British Museum, London.

ALFRED SISLEY (1839–99)

Born in Paris but of Anglo-French descent. Pupil of Charles Gleyre. Lived and worked as a landscape painter in Louveciennes, Marly-le-Roi, Sèvres, Veneux-Nadon and Moret-sur-Loing. Visited England and Wales to paint in 1874, 1881 and 1897. Exhibited in four of the Impressionist exhibitions (1874, 1876, 1877, 1882). Remained in financial distress for most of his life and died of cancer of the throat.

77. La Plaine de Thomery et le village de Champagne. 1875, or possibly 1876. Plate 70.
Black chalk. 28 × 40.7 cm. Dated: '1875' (or possibly '1876').
PROV: Paris, Durand-Ruel; Paris, Baron Louis de Chollet.
RELATED WORK: *La Plaine de Thomery et le village de Champagne*, oil, 1875–6 (D. 464 as *c.*1882).
Private Collection.

78. Drawing after 'La Seine au Point du Jour, fête du 30 juin 1878'. 1878. Plate 80.
Pen and ink. 15 × 24 cm. Signed: 'A. Sisley'.

LIT: Daulte, 1954, p. 58, no. 26; Daulte, 1972, p. 26; Thomson, 1981², p. 676. EXH: *Sisley*, 1981, no. 2.
RELATED WORKS: *La Seine au Point-du-Jour —le quatorze juillet*, oil, 1878 (D. 85); *La Seine au Point du Jour*, oil, 1878 (D. 295–8). Private Collection.

79. Portrait of the Artist's Son, Pierre. 1880. Plate 42.
Black chalk. 23 × 31 cm. Inscribed and dated centre below: 'Pierre 28 novembre/1880'.
PROV: Lady Kathleen Epstein/Sally Ryan, by whom presented, 1973 (GR. 237). LIT: Vigurs, 1976, p. 114; EXH: *Retrospective Alfred Sisley*, 1985, no. 54.
RELATED WORKS: *Head of a Boy (Pierre Sisley)*, black chalk, 1880 (Paris, Louvre, Cabinet des Dessins, inv. RF. 29655); *Study of Jeanne and Pierre Sisley*, pencil (Christie's, 6 December 1977, no. 117); *Study of Pierre Reading*, pencil (Christie's, 6 December 1977, no. 118); *Study of Pierre Reading*, pencil on grey paper (Christie's, 6 December 1977, no. 119); *Sheet of Studies of Pierre Playing Cards with the Painter Bouchor and of Mme Sisley*, pencil (Christie's, 6 December 1977, no. 120).
Lent by the Garman-Ryan Collection, Walsall Museum and Art Gallery.

80. Landscape with a Donkey at Saint-Mammès. *c.*1880–90. Plate 3.
Pastel. 26.7 × 33 cm. Signed lower right: 'Sisley'.
PROV: Glasgow, Sir William Burrell, acquired 1937; Glasgow, Burrell Collection (35/624).
Lent by The Burrell Collection, Glasgow Museums and Art Galleries.

FRANÇOIS-CLÉMENT SOMMIER, called HENRI SOMM (1844–1907)

Born in Rouen. By the late 1860s had established a reputation as an illustrator, caricaturist and designer. Much of his work was for fashionable journals such as *Le Monde Parisien* or *Tout-Paris*. Exhibited

with the Impressionists in 1879 only submitting two prints and a group of book illustrations. Friendship with Philippe Burty and Félix Braquemond led to the influence of *japonisme* in his work. Collaborated with Alfred Cadart.

81. The Beer Waitress (La Serveuse de bocks). *c.*1875–80. Plate 50.
Pencil, watercolour and gouache on buff paper. 24.2 × 15.9 cm. Signed lower right: 'Henri Somm'.
PROV: France, private collection; London, Hazlitt, Gooden and Fox, 1979. Private Collection.

JAMES JACQUES JOSEPH TISSOT (1836–1902)

Born at Nantes. Pupil of Lamothe and H. Flandrin. Influenced by Leys. Visited Italy and England during 1860s. Close friend of Degas and Whistler. Achieved considerable success in Paris Salon before outbreak of Franco-Prussian war (1870–1) and the Paris Commune (1871). Lived in London, 1871–82, and scored another notable success with portraits and scenes of contemporary life. After returning to France and visiting Palestine, 1886–7, concentrated on religious subjects winning widespread fame with his illustrations to the Bible. Died at Buillon near Besançon.

82. Study of a Standing Woman for 'The Captain and the Mate'. *c.*1873. Plate 75.
Gouache over black chalk on blue paper. 41.7 × 25.7 cm. Signed lower right: 'J. Tissot'.
PROV: purchased by the Ashmolean Museum, Oxford, 1942. LIT: Wentworth, 1984, p. 105. EXH: *James Tissot*, 1984–5, no. 63.
RELATED WORKS: *The Captain and the Mate*, oil, 1873 (private collection, England; Wentworth, pp. 31, 107); *Study of a Seated Woman*, gouache over black chalk on blue paper (Oxford, Ashmolean Museum; exh. London–Paris, 1984–5, no. 62).
Lent by the Visitors of The Ashmolean Museum, Oxford.

—————— Bibliography and Abbreviations ——————

The following bibliography is a selection of the works that the authors have found most useful in the preparation of this catalogue, with a deliberate emphasis on material dealing with works in British collections. Abbreviations used in the text and catalogue entries are indicated alongside the relevant items.

P. Adam, 'Peintres Impressionnistes', *Revue contemporaine*, 4, April–May 1886, 541–51.

J. Adhémar and F. Cachin, *Degas. The Complete Etchings, Lithographs, and Monotypes* (London, 1974).

J. Ajalbert, 'Le Salon des Impressionnistes', *La Revue moderne*, 30, 20 June 1886, 385–93.

R. Alley, *Catalogue of the Tate Gallery's Collection of Modern Art other than Works by British Artists* (London, 1981).

E.-E. Amaury-Duval, *L'Atelier d'Ingres* (2nd edn., Paris, 1924).

The Andrew Gow Collection, Cambridge, Fitwilliam Museum, 1978.

Selected Works from the Andrew Gow Bequest, London, Hazlitt, Gooden and Fox, 1978.

Anon. (H. Le Roux?), 'L'Exposition des Impressionnistes', *La République française*, 17 May 1886, 3.

Archives de Camille Pissarro, Paris, Hôtel Drouot, 21 November 1975.

A. Baignères, 'Société d'Aquarellistes Français (Première Exposition)', *Gazette des Beaux-Arts*, 29 May 1879, 491–501.

A. Baignères, 'Société d'Aquarellistes Français (Quatrième Exposition)', *Gazette des Beaux-Arts*, 25 April 1882, 433–9.

G. Ballas, 'Daumier, Corot, Papety et Delacroix, inspirateurs de Cézanne', *Bulletin de la Société de l'Histoire de l'Art Français*, 1974, 193–9.

G. Ballas, 'Paul Cézanne et la Revue "L'Artiste"', *Gazette des Beaux-Arts*, 98, December 1981, 223–31.

[B/W] M.-L. Bataille and G. Wildenstein, *Berthe Morisot. Catalogue des Peintures, Pastels et Aquarelles* (Paris, 1961).

C. Baudelaire, *Art in Paris, 1845–62. Salons and other Exhibitions Reviewed by Charles Baudelaire*, trans. and ed. J. Mayne (London, 1965).

L. Bénédite, *Albert Lebourg* (Paris, 1923).

G. Besson, *Signac Dessins* (Paris, 1950).

C. Bigot, 'L'Exposition des Impressionnistes', *La Revue politique et littéraire*, 28 April 1877, 1045–8.

J.-E. Blanche, *Propos de Peintre. De David à Degas* (Paris, 1919).

E. Blot, *Histoire d'une collection de tableaux modernes* (Paris, 1934).

M. Bodelsen, *Gauguin's Ceramics* (London, 1964).

M. Bodelsen, 'Early Impressionist sales, 1874–94, in the light of some unpublished "procès-verbaux"', *Burlington Magazine*, 110, June 1968, 331–49.

M. Bodelsen, 'Gauguin the Collector', *Burlington Magazine*, 112, September 1970, 590–615.

A. Boime, 'The Salon des Refusés and the Evolution of Modern Art', *Art Quarterly*, 32, 1969, 411–26.

A. Boime, *The Academy and French Painting in the Nineteenth Century* (London, 1971).

A. Boime, 'Entrepreneurial Patronage in Nineteenth Century France', in E. Carter, R. Forster and J. Moody (eds.), *Enterprise and Entrepreneurs in 19th and 20th Century France* (Baltimore, 1976) 137–207.

A. Boime, 'The Teaching Reforms of 1863 and the Origins of Modernism', *Art Quarterly*, NS I, 1977, 1–39.

A. Boime, *Thomas Couture and the Eclectic Vision* (London and New Haven, 1980).

M.-C. Boucher, *Musée du Petit Palais. Catalogue des dessins et peintures de Puvis de Chavannes* (Paris, 1979).

M.-C. Boucher and D. Imbert, *Musée du Petit Palais. Catalogue sommaire illustré des pastels* (Paris, 1983).

Boudin. Aquarelles et Pastels, Paris, Musée du Louvre, Cabinet des Dessins, 1965.

F. Bracquemond, *Du dessin et de la couleur* (Paris, 1885).

[B/L] R. Brettell and C. Lloyd, *A Catalogue of the Drawings by Camille Pissarro in The Ashmolean Museum, Oxford* (Oxford, 1980).

N. Broude, 'The Influence of Rembrandt Reproductions on Seurat's Drawing Style: A Methodological Note', *Gazette des Beaux-Arts*, 88, October 1976, 155–60.

L. Browse, *Degas Dancers* (London, 1949).

Félix Buhot, Peintre-Graveur. Prints, Drawings and Paintings, Minneapolis Institute of Arts, 1983–4, subsequently Baltimore Museum of Art, the Fine Arts Museums of San Francisco.

A. Callen, *Techniques of the Impressionists* (London, 1982).

A. Carel, *Les Brasseries à femmes de Paris* (Paris, 1884).

Cent Dessins Français du Fitzwilliam Museum, Cambridge, Paris, Galerie Heim, 1976, subsequently Lille, Palais des Beaux-Arts, Strasbourg, Musée des Beaux-Arts.

Centenaire de l'Impressionnisme, Paris, Grand Palais, 1974, subsequently New York, Metropolitan Museum of Art.

Paul Cézanne Aquarelle, Kunsthalle Tübingen, 1982, subsequently Zurich,

Kunsthaus.

D. Chambers, *Notes on a Selection of Woodblocks by Lucien Pissarro held at the Ashmolean Museum* (Oxford, 1980).

A. Chappuis, *The Drawings of Paul Cézanne. A Catalogue Raisonné* (2 vols., London, 1973).

L. Chardin, 'Salon Illustré de 1879', *L'Artiste*, 11, December 1879, 421–6.

J. Claretie, *La Vie à Paris, 1880* (Paris, 1881).

B. R. Collins, 'Manet's *Rue Mosnier Decked with Flags* and the Flâneur Concept', *Burlington Magazine*, 117, November 1975, 709–14.

D. Cooper, *Pastels by Degas* (London, 1952).

D. Cooper, *The Courtauld Collection. A Catalogue and Introduction* (London, 1954).

Correspondance de Berthe Morisot, ed. D. Rouart (Paris, 1950).

Correspondance de Camille Pissarro, I, 1865–1885, ed. J. Bailly-Herzberg (Paris, 1980).

The Crisis of Impressionism, 1878–1882, the University of Michigan Museum of Art, 1979–80.

F. Daulte, *Le Dessin français de Manet à Cézanne* (Lausanne and Paris, 1954).

F. Daulte, *Pierre-Auguste Renoir. Aquarelle, Pastelle und farbige Zeichnungen* (Stuttgart, 1958).

[D] F. Daulte, *Alfred Sisley. Catalogue raisonné de l'œuvre peint* (Lausanne, 1959).

F. Daulte, *Auguste Renoir. Catalogue raisonné de l'œuvre peint, I, Figures, 1860–1890* (Lausanne, 1971).

F. Daulte, *Sisley* (Milan, 1972).

Degas Monotypes, Cambridge (Mass.), Fogg Art Museum, 1968.

Degas, Pastels and Drawings, Nottingham University Art Gallery, 1969.

Degas, 1879, Edinburgh, National Gallery of Scotland, 1979.

Edgar Degas, 1834–1917, London, David Carritt Ltd., 1983.

Degas. Pastelle, Ölskizzen, Zeichnungen, Kunsthalle Tübingen, 1984, subsequently Berlin, Nationalgalerie.

Edgar Degas: The Painter as Printmaker, Boston Museum of Fine Arts, 1984–5, subsequently Philadelphia Museum of Art, London, Hayward Gallery.

Degas e l'Italia, Rome, Villa Medici, 1984–5.

Degas: The Dancers, Washington, National Gallery of Art, 1984–5.

H. Delaborde, *Ingres, sa vie, ses travaux, sa doctrine* (Paris, 1870).

From Delacroix to Cézanne. French Water-colour Landscapes of the Nineteenth Century, University of Maryland Art Gallery, 1977–8, subsequently Louisville, J. B. Speed Art Museum; University of Michigan Museum of Art.

L. Delteil, *Le Peintre-Graveur illustré*, XXVII. *Camille Pissarro, Alfred Sisley, Auguste Renoir* (Paris, 1923).

Les Dessins de Georges Seurat, Paris, 1926.

[D/R] H. Dorra and J. Rewald, *Seurat. L'Oeuvre peint. Biographie et catalogue critique* (Paris, 1959).

Drawing, Technique and Purpose, London, Victoria and Albert Museum, 1981.

Drawings from the Collection of Louis C. G. Clarke LL D, 1881–1960, Cambridge, Fitzwilliam Museum, 1981–2.

Drawings from the National Gallery of Ireland, London, Wildenstein, 1967.

E. Duranty, *La Nouvelle Peinture* (Paris, 1876).

Dürer to Cézanne: Northern European Drawings from The Ashmolean Museum, the Jane Voorhees Zimmerli Art Museum, Rutgers University, 1982, subsequently Cleveland, The Cleveland Museum of Art.

T. Duret, *Histoire d'Edouard Manet et de son œuvre . . ., avec un catalogue des peintures et des pastels* (Paris, 1902).

J. Elderfield, 'Drawing in Cézanne', *Art Forum*, IX, June 1971, 51–7.

C. Ephrussi, 'Exposition des artistes indé-pendants', *Gazette des Beaux-Arts*, 21, May 1880, 485–8.

European Drawings from the Fitzwilliam, New York, Pierpont Morgan Library, 1976–7, subsequently Fort Worth, Kimbell Art Museum; Minneapolis Institute of Arts; Philadelphia Museum of Art.

C. Fehrer, 'New Light on the Académie Julian and its Founder (Rodolphe Julian)', *Gazette des Beaux-Arts*, 103, May/June 1984, 207–16.

F. Fénéon, *Oeuvres plus que complètes*, ed. J. U. Halperin (2 vols., Geneva, 1970).

H. Fèvre, 'L'Exposition des Impression-nistes', *Revue de Demain*, May/June 1886, 148–56.

A. Fontaine, *Conférences inédites de l'Académie Royale de Peinture et de Sculpture d'après les manuscrits des ar-chives de l'École des Beaux-Arts* (Paris, n.d. (1903)).

B. Foucart, *Débats et polémiques à propos de l'enseignement des arts du dessin. Louis Vitet, Eugène Viollet-le-Duc* (Paris, 1984).

L. de Fourcaud, 'Le Salon de 1884', *Gazette des Beaux-Arts*, 30, August 1884, 105–21.

The Frick Collection. An Illustrated Catalogue. Vol. II. Paintings. French, Italian and Spanish (New York, 1960).

S. Gache-Patin, 'Douze œuvres de Cézanne de l'ancienne collection Pellerin', *Revue du Louvre*, 34, 1984, 128–46.

Paul Gauguin. Carnet de croquis, ed. J. Rewald and R. Cogniat (New York, 1962).

Gauguin and the Pont-Aven Group, London, Tate Gallery, 1966.

Paul Gauguin; The Writings of a Savage, ed. D. Guérin (New York, 1978).

G. Geffroy, 'Hors du Salon. Les Impressionnistes', *La Justice*, 26 May 1886, n.p.

M. Gerstein, 'Degas's Fans', *Art Bulletin*, 64, March 1982, 105–18.

F. Gibson, *The Art of Henri Fantin-Latour: His Life and Work* (London, 1924).

P. Gilbert, 'Chronique. Exposition des pas-tellistes', *Journal des Artistes*, 25 April 1886, 129.

Glasgow Art Gallery. Catalogue of French Paintings (Glasgow, 1953).

Charles Gleyre ou les illusions perdues, Winterthur, Kunstmuseum, 1974–5, subsequently Marseilles, Musée Cantini; Munich, Stadtliche Galerie im Lenbachhaus; Kiel, Kunsthaus; Aarau, Aargauer Kunsthaus; Lausanne, Musée Cantonal des Beaux-Arts.

Charles Gleyre, 1806–1874, New York University, Grey Art Gallery, 1980, subsequently University of Maryland Art Gallery.

E. and J. de Goncourt, *Journal. Mémoires de la vie littéraire*, ed. R. Ricatte (22 vols., Monaco, 1956).

C. Gottlieb, 'Boudin's Drawings', *Master Drawings*, 6, no. 4, 1968, 395–404.

C. Gray, *Armand Guillaumin* (Chester, Conn., 1972).

T. A. Gronberg, 'Femmes de brasserie', *Art History*, 7, September 1984, 329–44.

P. Grunchec, *Le Grand Prix de peinture. Les concours des Prix de Rome de 1797 à 1863* (Paris, 1983).

M. Guérin, *L'Œuvre gravé de Manet* (Paris, 1944).

M. Hamel, 'A French Artist: Léon Lhermitte (1844–1925)', (Ph.D. thesis, Washington University, 1974).

J. C. Harris, *Edouard Manet: Graphic Works, a Definitive Catalogue Raisonné* (New York, 1970).

[DH] C. de Hauke, *Seurat et son œuvre* (2 vols., Paris, 1961).

H. Havard, 'L'Exposition des Artistes Indépendants', *Le Siècle*, 27 April 1879, 3.

G. Heard Hamilton, *Manet and his Critics* (New York, 1954).

V. Hefting, *Jongkind, sa vie, son œuvre, son époque* (Paris, 1975).

R. L. Herbert, *Seurat's Drawings* (New York, 1962).

E. d'Hervilly, 'Exposition des Impressionnistes', *Le Rappel*, 11 April 1879, 2.

P. H. Hulton, *The César Mange de Hauke Bequest* (London, 1968).

H. R. Hoetinck, *Franse Tekeningen uit de 19e Eeuw. Catalogus van de verzameling in het Museum Boymans-van Beuningen* (Rotterdam, 1968).

Œuvres complètes de J.-K. Huysmans, vol. VI, L'Art Moderne, vol. X, Certains (Paris, 1929).

Impressionism. Its Masters, its Precursors, and its Influence in Britain, London, the Royal Academy of Art, 1974.

The Impressionists and the Post-Impressionists from the Courtauld Collection, University of London, Tokyo, Takashimaya, 1984, subsequently Kyoto, Takashimaya; Osaka, Takashimaya.

J. Ingamells, *The Davies Collection of French Art* (Cardiff, 1967).

J.-A.-D. Ingres, *Réponse au rapport sur l'École imperiale des Beaux-Arts* (Paris, 1863).

J. Isaacson, *Claude Monet. Observation and Reflection* (Oxford, 1978).

P. Jamot and G. Wildenstein, *Manet* (2 vols., Paris, 1933).

G. Kahn, *Les Dessins de Georges Seurat* (2 vols., Paris, 1928).

R. Kendall (ed.), *Degas, 1834–1984* (Manchester, 1985).

Œuvres complètes de Jules Laforgue, IV, Lettres, I, 1881–1882, ed. G. Jean-Aubry (Paris, 1925).

Exposition Lebourg, Paris, Galerie Georges Petit, 1918.

G. Lecomte, *L'Art Impressionniste* (Paris, 1892).

H. Lecoq de Boisbaudran, *The Training of the Memory in Art and the Education of the Artist . . .*, trans. L. D. Luard with an intro. by S. Image (London, 1911).

A. de Leiris, *The Drawings of Édouard Manet* (Berkeley and Los Angeles, 1969).

[L] P.-A. Lemoisne, *Degas et son œuvre* (4 vols., Paris, 1946–9); *Supplement* by P. Brame, T. Reff and A. Reff (New York and London, 1984).

P.-A. Lemoisne, *Degas et son œuvre* (Paris, 1954).

S. Lichtenstein, 'Cézanne and Delacroix', *Art Bulletin*, 46, March 1964, 55–67, 425–6.

S. Lichtenstein, 'Cézanne's Copies and Variants after Delacroix', *Apollo*, 101, February 1975, 116–27.

C. Lloyd, 'Nineteenth Century French Drawings in the Bryson Bequest to the Ashmolean Museum', *Master Drawings*, 16, no. 3, 1978, 284–7.

C. Lloyd, 'Camille Pissarro: Drawings or Prints', *Master Drawings*, 18, no. 3, 1980, 264–8.

C. Lloyd, *Pissarro* (Geneva, 1981).

C. Lloyd, 'The Market Scenes of Camille Pissarro', *Art Bulletin of Victoria*, 25, 1985, 16–32.

A. de Lostalot, Exposition des Artistes Indépendants, *Les Beaux-Arts Illustrés*, 10, 1879, 82–3.

A. de Lostalot, review of Henry de Chennevières, *Les Dessins du Louvre*, *Gazette des Beaux-Arts*, 26, August 1882, 173–7.

[Lugt] F. Lugt, *Les Marques de collections de dessins et d'estampes*, Amsterdam (1921), *Supplément* (The Hague, 1956).

G. Mack, *Paul Cézanne* (Paris, n.d. (1935)).

Édouard Manet. L'œuvre gravé, Chefs d'œuvre du Département des Estampes de la Bibliothèque Nationale, Paris (Ingelheim am Rhein, 1977).

Manet: dessins, aquarelles, eaux-fortes, lithographies, correspondance, Paris, Huguette Berès, 1978.

Manet at Work, London, National Gallery, 1983.

Manet. 1832–1883, Paris, Grand Palais, 1983, subsequently New York, Metropolitan Museum.

Mantegna to Cézanne. Master Drawings from the Courtauld, London, British Museum, 1983.

D. Martelli, *Les Impressionnistes et l'Art Moderne*, ed. F. Errico (Paris, 1979).

Master Drawings and Watercolours in the British Museum, ed. J. Rowlands (London, 1984).

J. Mathey, *Graphisme de Manet. II. Peintures réapparues* (Paris, 1963).

P.-L. Mathieu, *Gustave Moreau* (Oxford, 1977).

J. Meier-Graefe, *Edouard Manet* (Munich, 1912).

A. Michel, 'L'Exposition des dessins du siècle', *Gazette des Beaux-Arts*, 29, March 1884, 220–9; April 1884, 314–26.

J. Millet, 'La Famille Mante, Une Trichromie, Degas, l'Opéra', *Gazette des*

Beaux-Arts, 94, October 1979, 105–12.

O. Mirbeau, 'Exposition de peinture. I, rue Laffitte', *La France*, 21 May 1886, 1–2.

O. Mirbeau, *Des Artistes, I* (Paris, 1922).

G. Monnier, *Pastels. From the 16th to the 20th Century* (Geneva, 1984).

E. Moreau-Nélaton, *Jongkind raconté par lui-même* (Paris, 1918).

M. J. Moynet, *L'Envers du Théâtre. Machines et Décorations* (2nd edn., Paris, 1874).

C. Nathanson and E. Olszewski, 'Degas's Angel of the Apocalypse', *Bulletin of the Cleveland Museum of Art*, 67, October 1980, 243–55.

Paper. An Exhibition of works by Degas, Renoir, Pissarro, Van Gogh, Vuillard, Cézanne, Valtat, Redon, Léger, Matisse, Moore, Bonnard, Giacometti, Dubuffet, Picasso, Balthus, London, Thomas Gibson Fine Art Ltd., 1985.

K. T. Parker, *Catalogue of the Collection of Drawings in The Ashmolean Museum. Volume I. Netherlandish, German, French and Spanish Schools* (Oxford, 1938).

The Peasant in French 19th Century Art, Dublin, The Douglas Hyde Gallery, Trinity College, 1980.

N. Pevsner, *Academies of Art Past and Present* (Cambridge, 1940).

R. Pickvance, 'Drawings by Degas in English Public Collections, Parts I–IV', *The Connoisseur*, 157, October/ November 1964, 82–3, 162–3; 159, July/August 1965, 158–9, 228–9.

R. Pickvance, 'Some Aspects of Degas's Nudes', *Apollo*, 83, January 1966, 17–23.

R. Pickvance, *Gauguin Drawings* (London, 1970).

C. Pissarro, *Lettres à son fils Lucien*, ed. J. Rewald (Paris, 1950).

Pissarro in England, London, Marlborough Fine Art, 1968.

Camille Pissarro, 1830–1903, London, Hayward Gallery, 1980–1, subsequently Paris, Grand Palais; Boston, Museum of Fine Arts.

[P & V] L. R. Pissarro and L. Venturi, *Camille Pissarro. Son art—son œuvre* (2 vols., Paris, 1939).

Post-Impressionism. Cross-currents in European Painting, London, Royal Academy, 1979–80.

G. Privat, 'Les Aquarellistes', *L'Artiste*, March 1881, 355–7.

J. Puget, *La Vie extraordinaire de Forain* (Paris, 1957).

In Pursuit of Perfection: The Art of J.-A.-D. Ingres, Louisville, J. B. Speed Art Museum, 1983–4, subsequently Fort Worth, Kimbell Art Museum.

Puvis de Chavannes, 1824–1898, Paris, Grand Palais, 1977, subsequently Ottawa, National Gallery of Canada.

The Realist Tradition. French Painting and Drawing, 1830–1900, Cleveland, The Cleveland Museum of Art, 1980–2, subsequently New York, The Brooklyn Museum; St. Louis, St. Louis Art Museum; Glasgow, Glasgow Art Gallery and Museum.

T. Reff, 'Cézanne's Drawings, 1875–85', *Burlington*, 101, May 1959, 171–6.

T. Reff, 'Reproductions and Books in Cézanne's Studio', *Gazette des Beaux-Arts*, 56, November 1960, 303–9.

T. Reff, 'Degas's Copies of Older Art', *Burlington*, 105, June 1963, 241–51.

T. Reff, 'New Light on Degas's Copies', *Burlington*, 106, June 1964, 250–9.

T. Reff, 'Copyists in the Louvre', *Art Bulletin*, 46, December 1964, 552–9.

T. Reff, 'Addenda on Degas's Copies', *Burlington Magazine*, 107, June 1965, 320–3.

T. Reff, 'Further Thoughts on Degas's Copies', *Burlington Magazine*, 113, September 1971, 534–43.

T. Reff, *The Notebooks of Edgar Degas* (2 vols., Oxford, 1976).

T. Reff, 'Cézanne's *Cardplayers* and their Sources', *Arts Magazine*, 55, November 1980, 104–17.

T. Reff, *Modern Art in Paris. Two Hundred Catalogues of the Major Exhibitions Reproduced in Facsimile in Forty-seven Volumes. Impressionist Group Exhibitions* (New York and London, 1981).

Renoir: Carnet de dessins—Renoir en Italie et en Algérie, pref. A. André, intro. G. Besson (Paris, 1955).

Retrospective Camille Pissarro, Tokyo, Isetan Museum of Art, 1984, subsequently Fukuoka Art Museum; Kyoto Municipal Museum of Art.

Retrospective Alfred Sisley, Tokyo, Isetan Museum of Art, 1985, subsequently Fukuoka Art Museum; Nara Prefectural Museum.

J. Rewald, 'Auguste Renoir and his Brother', *Gazette des Beaux-Arts*, 27, March 1945, 171–88.

J. Rewald, *Renoir Drawings* (New York, 1946).

J. Rewald, *Gauguin Drawings* (New York, 1958).

J. Rewald, *The History of Impressionism* (4th edn., London, 1973).

J. Rewald, 'Theo Van Gogh, Goupil, and the Impressionists', *Gazette des Beaux-Arts*, 41, January 1973, 1–64; February 1973, 65–108.

J. Rewald, *Paul Cézanne: The Watercolours. A Catalogue Raisonné* (London, 1984).

[R/W] D. Rouart and D. Wildenstein, *Edouard Manet, catalogue raisonné*, (2 vols., Lausanne and Paris, 1975).

R. Saisselin, *Bricabracomania. The Bourgeois and the Bibelot* (London, 1985).

R. Schmit, *Eugène Boudin* (3 vols., Paris, 1973).

Georges Seurat, Paris, Bernheim Jeune, 1920.

Alfred Sisley, 1839–1899, David Carritt Ltd., London 1981.

Société d'Aquarellistes Français. Ouvrage d'Art (2 vols., Paris, 1883).

W. Stechow, *Catalogue of Drawings and Watercolours in the Allen Memorial Art Museum, Oberlin College* (Oberlin, 1976).

H. Sutton, *The Life and Work of Jean Richepin* (Geneva, 1961).

A. Tabarant, *Manet et ses œuvres* (Paris, 1947).

P. ten-Doesschate Chu, 'Lecoq de Boisbaudran and Memory Drawing. A Teaching Course between Idealism and Naturalism', in G. P. Weisberg (ed.), *The European Realist Tradition* (Indiana University Press, 1982), 242–89.

R. Thomson, 'Drawings by Camille Pissarro in Manchester Public Collections', *Master Drawings*, 18, no. 3, 1980, 257–63.

R. Thomson, *French Nineteenth Century Drawings in the Whitworth Art Gallery* (Manchester, 1981[1]).

R. Thomson, 'A Sisley problem', *Burlington Magazine*, 123, November 1981[2], 676.

R. Thomson, 'The Sculpture of Camille Pissarro', *Source*, 11, Summer 1983, 25–8.

R. Thomson, *Seurat* (Oxford, 1985).

James Tissot (1836–1902). An Exhibition of Paintings, Drawings and Etchings, Sheffield, Graves Art Gallery, 1955.

James Tissot, London, Barbican Art Gallery, 1984–5, subsequently Manchester, Whitworth Art Gallery; Paris, Petit Palais.

Treasures from the Burrell Collection, London, Hayward Gallery, 1975.

P. Tucker, 'The First Impressionist Exhibition and Monet's *Impression, Sunrise*; a Tale of Timing, Commerce and Patriotism', *Art History*, 7, December 1984, 465–76.

O. Uzanne, *L'Éventail* (Paris, 1882).

M. Vachon, *Puvis de Chavannes* (Paris, 1900).

P. Valéry, *Degas, Danse, Dessin* (Paris, 1936).

[V] L. Venturi, *Cézanne. Son art—son œuvre* (2 vols., Paris, 1936).

L. Venturi, *Les Archives de l'Impressionnisme* (2 vols., Paris, 1939).

U. de Vielcastel, 'Le Pastel et le dix-huitième siècle', *L'Artiste*, April 1881, 435–7.

P. Vigurs, *The Garman-Ryan Collection. Illustrated Catalogue* (Walsall, 1976).

E. Viollet-le-Duc, 'L'enseignement des arts—il y a quelque chose', *Gazette des Beaux-Arts*, 12, May 1862, 393–402, June 1862, 525–34; 13, July 1862, 71–82, September 1862, 249–55.

E. Viollet-le-Duc, *Réponse à M. Vitet à propos de l'enseignement des arts du dessin* (Paris, 1864).

L. Vitet, 'Les arts du dessin en France', *Revue des Deux Mondes*, 1 November 1864, 74–107.

A. Vollard, *Degas Album* (Paris, 1914).

A. Vollard, *Tableaux, pastels et dessins de Pierre-Auguste Renoir* (2 vols., Paris, 1918).

A. Vollard, *La Vie et l'œuvre de Pierre-Auguste Renoir* (Paris, 1919).

A. Vollard, *Degas* (Paris, 1924).

N. Wadley, 'Cézanne Water-colours and Drawings at the Hayward Gallery', *Burlington Magazine*, 115, 1973, 831–2.

Watercolour and Pencil Drawings by Cézanne, Newcastle upon Tyne, Laing Art Gallery, 1973, subsequently London, Hayward Gallery.

J. Wechsler, 'An Apéritif to Manet's *Déjeuner sur l'Herbe*', *Gazette des Beaux-Arts*, 91, January 1978, 32–4.

M. Wentworth, *James Tissot* (Oxford, 1984).

B. E. White, 'Renoir's Trip to Italy', *Art Bulletin*, 51, December 1969, 333–51.

B. E. White, 'The *Bathers* of 1887 and Renoir's Anti-Impressionism', *Art Bulletin*, 55, March 1973, 106–26.

P. A. Wick, 'Degas's Violinist', *Bulletin of the Museum of Fine Arts, Boston*, 57, 1959, 87–101.

D. Wildenstein, *Claude Monet. Biographie et catalogue raisonné. I. 1840–1881, II. 1882–1886, III. 1887–1898* (Lausanne and Paris, 1974–9).

G. Wildenstein, 'Un carnet des dessins de Sisley au Musée du Louvre', *Gazette des Beaux-Arts*, 53, January 1959, 57–60.

[W] G. Wildenstein, *Gauguin. I. Catalogue* (Paris, 1964).

A. Wolff (pref.), *J.-F. Raffaëlli, Les Types de Paris* (Paris, 1889).

Index

ACKNOWLEDGEMENTS

The Arts Council and publishers are grateful to all those institutions and individuals who have supplied photographic material for this catalogue or have given permission for its use, in particular to the British Rail Pension Funds Works of Art Collection (Figs. 13, 27); Harvard University Art Museums (The Fogg Art Museum) Anonymous Gift in memory of W. G. Russell Allen (Fig. 2); the National Gallery of Art, Washington, Chester Dale Collection (Fig. 37); the National Gallery of Art, Washington, Gift of the W. Averell Harriman Foundation in memory of Marie N. Harriman (Fig. 47); the Oeffentliche Kunstsammlung Basel, Dr h. c. Emile Dreyfus-Fondation (Fig. 43). Thanks are also due to the following for photographing individual works: James Austin (Plate 67), John Cass (Plates 24, 30, 61, 62); and Dave Gross (Plates 69, 77).